THE
PEASANTS'
REVOLT

THE
PEASANTS' REVOLT

ENGLAND'S FAILED REVOLUTION OF

1381

ALASTAIR DUNN

TEMPUS

Cover illustration: The death of Wat Tyler, Roy. 18.E.I fl75.
By permission of The British Library

First published 2002 as *The Great Rising of 1381*
This edition first published 2004

Tempus Publishing Limited
The Mill, Brimscombe Port,
Stroud, Gloucestershire, GL5 2QG

ISBN 0 7524 2965 5

Typesetting and origination by Tempus Publishing Limited
Printed and bound in the USA

CONTENTS

ACKNOWLEDGEMENTS

I have incurred a number of debts when writing this book. Jonathan Reeve of Tempus Publishing steered this book from its earliest stages through to its completion, and was never lacking in encouragement and enthusiasm. Joanna de Vries converted the manuscript into a proof with speed and efficiency.

At St Andrews Chris Given-Wilson, John Hudson, Ann Kettle, Robert Bartlett, and David Green helped me in many ways. Tony Goodman allowed me to pick his brains on his deep knowledge of fourteenth-century England, and told me things that I should have known already. However, any errors in this book are the author's own.

Edward Heaton, Christopher Howarth and Nicolas and Lucy Jackson offered me their hospitality during trips to London, and I owe them my thanks. Richard Bray of Luvians helped to educate my palate. Finally, my parents have supported me throughout the writing of this book, which is dedicated to them with love and thanks.

St Andrews
April 2002

PREFACE

In revising this work for a second edition I have attempted to expand on various areas that received less than full treatment in *The Great Rising of 1381*. In particular I have taken the story of the war with France back to 1369, and have considered the cumulative impact of the military defeats and diplomatic humiliations that ensued over the following decade. I have also attempted to bring in more contextual detail to the consideration of the changing state of rural society in the century before 1381. Thirdly, I have drawn upon some recently published research to further illustrate the broad social composition of The Rising. Otherwise, I have left the main narrative of this work unchanged, especially in the sections relating to the rebel occupation of London.

As before, this is dedicated to my parents, with love and thanks.

AJD
June 2004

London and its Suburbs in 1381

For the details of this map, I am indebted to C. Oman, *The Great Revolt* and C. Barron, *The Revolt in London* .

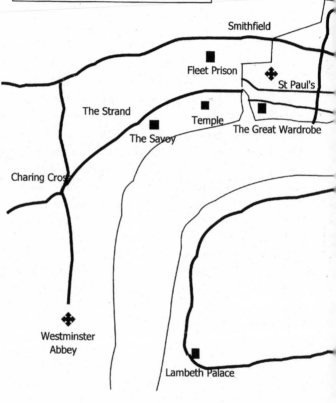

Clerkenwell

Priory of St John

Smithfield

Fleet Prison

St Paul's

The Strand

Temple

The Great Wardrobe

The Savoy

Charing Cross

Westminster Abbey

Lambeth Palace

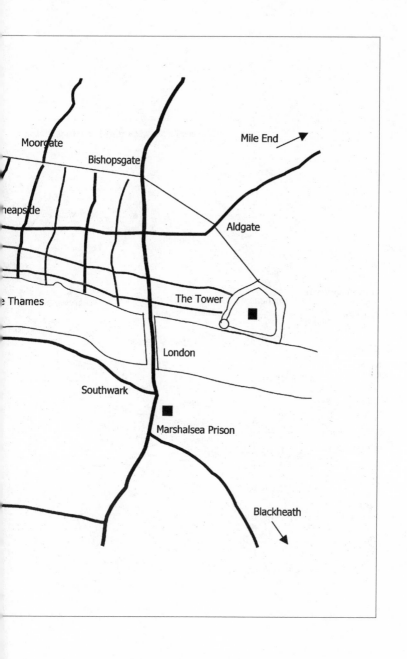

Moorgate

Bishopsgate

Cheapside

Mile End

Aldgate

The Thames

The Tower

London

Southwark

Marshalsea Prison

Blackheath

Eastern England During The Great Rising

Lincolnshire

Rutland

Norfolk

Baconsthorpe

North Walsham

Norwich

Yarmouth

Stamford

Ely

Lynn

Huntingdonshire

Cambridgeshire

Lakenheath

Suffolk

Mettingham Castle

Northamptonshire

Huntingdon

Cambridge

Bury St Edmunds

Framlingham

Bedfordshire

Bedford

Hertfordshire

Cressing

Colchester

St Albans

Essex

Barnet

Brentwood

Billericay

Middlesex

Havering atte Bower

Fobbing

London

Blackheath

Rochester

Surrey

Kent

Canterbury

Tonbridge

Maidstone

Sussex

THE RURAL WORLD OF THE FOURTEENTH CENTURY

RURAL ECONOMY AND SOCIETY BEFORE THE BLACK DEATH, *c.*1250–1349

In June and July 1381 the towns and counties of southern and eastern England experienced the most significant outbreak of popular protest in British history. Later rebellions, such as the religious protests of the mid-sixteenth century, may have touched more parts of the kingdom, while the mass civil actions of the nineteenth and twentieth centuries certainly attracted more participants in absolute terms, but none of these has a historical significance to match that of 1381. Perhaps 1381 continues to stand out because it was undoubtedly the first major popular rising, in which participants from across the kingdom shared enough points of grievance (albeit with significant local variations) to justify its classification as a national revolt. Unlike many later disturbances, which had no immediately discernible start and end points, that of 1381 has a remarkable and fairly self-contained chronology. There were no warning tremors and no aftershocks of any significance, although popular protest did recur, albeit on a smaller scale, in the second half of the fifteenth century. But perhaps the enduring fame of the 1381 revolt can be found in the remarkable cast of characters involved, the impressive backdrops and the dramatic set-piece encounters, especially during the phase of rebel occupation of London. Undoubtedly there is a dramatic quality to the revolt, and the leading characters, both rebels and royalists alike, are thrown into sharp relief by the events unfolding around them. The modern understanding of 1381 owes much to the survival of a remarkable body of contemporary narratives, each of which brings its own perspectives and prejudices. These sources cannot be used uncritically, and their attempts at characterisation, especially through quoted direct speech, must be treated with caution. But, to discard these admittedly troublesome sources would be to strip out the core narrative of what is undoubtedly one of the most exciting events of British history. Medieval chroniclers had a tendency to fabricate, to omit inconvenient facts and even to knowingly distort the order of events, but their very flaws add colour and texture to an event that polarised the opinions of contemporaries to an extraordinary degree.

In spite of the efforts of historians to emphasise the broader political, economic and military dimensions behind the events of 1381, and the diverse origins of its participants, the rising is still commonly known as 'The Peasants' Revolt'. This is partly due to the hostile chroniclers, who called the rebels 'rustici', an expression which had powerful connotations of backwardness and ignorance. But, the rebels called themselves 'the king's true commons', and would probably never have used the French word 'peasant'. When called upon to do so (for example in a law court) the medieval commoner would have supplied a self-description from his or her occupation, social status, or relationship to a superior, while the mass of ordinary people were collectively called 'the commons' or 'the men of the country' (by which was usually meant the *county*). The term 'peasant' has more meaning as a term of classification imposed by modern social and economic historians, and is better suited to the rural societies of medieval France and Germany, and more especially to that of post-medieval Eastern Europe. Significantly, the German 'Bauernkrieg' of the 1520s is commonly known in English as 'The Peasants' War'. Therefore, given its continuing popularity, it seems likely that 'The Peasants' Revolt' will endure as the commonly used description for the events of 1381. In this respect, the literate church chroniclers will have achieved a very long-lasting victory over the predominantly illiterate rebels.

THE SOCIAL HIERARCHY OF THE MEDIEVAL COUNTRYSIDE

Long before the Conquest of 1066 the English countryside had been dominated by a political elite that derived its authority from the control of land and agricultural production. After 1066 this elite was replaced by a French-speaking military nobility, which carved up the countryside as tenants of the Norman kings and constructed castles (at first from wood and later from stone) for the administration and defence of their estates. This tier of Norman, French and Flemish barons consolidated its lordship through dynastic alliances, and many married into the surviving remnant of the lesser nobility of Anglo-Saxon England. Through granting estates to their own tenants, servants and followers, the twelfth and thirteenth century nobility created an elaborate web of lordship and tenancy, political leadership and economic inter-dependency. By the thirteenth century a knightly class had come to imitate the lifestyles and tastes of their superiors, adopting personal heraldry and channelling the wealth that they could spare into the building of stone manor houses and the enlargement of their parish churches.

Of course much of the landed wealth of England had been in the hands of the bishoprics and abbeys long before the Conquest. After 1066, patronage of the church by kings and nobles alike flourished for more than two centuries. Some of the Anglo-Saxon bishoprics were relocated to the sites where the great Norman and Gothic cathedrals survive to this day, but perhaps the most striking phenomenon of this period was the proliferation of abbeys and priories founded by the new nobility, and endowed by them with great estates. Thus, the acquisition, cultivation and enlargement of landed estates was a central pre-occupation of the lay and ecclesiastical elites, reflected in the explosion of record-keeping from the second half of the twelfth century, and also in the emergence of treatises on husbandry, accounting and household management.

But beneath the level of the French-speaking nobility and their immediate tenants, there was a continuity of rural habitation by the English-speaking descendants of earlier Saxon and Norse settlers. England under the Conqueror and his successors was a well settled kingdom, and had long been divided into counties, hundreds and other local, customary sub-divisions. In the southern half of the kingdom settlement was often dense, while some of the market towns and ports had been in existence since the period of Roman occupation. But in spite of the growth of urban settlements up to the middle of the fourteenth century, England remained an essentially rural society, and about eighty-ninety per cent of the population lived in the countryside. Even among the poorer tenant farmers of the eleventh, twelfth and thiteenth centuries there was a considerable variety of living standards, as evidenced by the differing sizes of holdings and the conditions of their tenure.

England's agrarian landscape in the thirteenth and fourteenth centuries contained significant boundaries. The midland and south-central counties were characterised by the open-field system, in which arable cultivation was carried out by households grouped together in plough teams. Typically, this extended region supported large and well developed villages. But the counties immediately south and east of London (which were particularly affected by the 1381 revolt) had different patterns of settlement. Essex had traditionally been dominated by royal forest, while the East Anglian counties were distinguished by early enclosures and a high incidence of crafts and cottage industry.[1] The wooded areas East of London also tended to contain smaller and more scattered hamlets rather than the larger villages typical of the south midlands.[2] In spite of these regional differences in agricultural practice before the Black Death, there were enough common features to permit some tentative generalisations about the landed holdings of typical tenant families. The peasant dwelling, known as the messuage, existed in varying shapes and sizes, depending on a number of factors, including the wealth of the family and the size of the holding that supported it. Christopher Dyer has identified substantial peasant dwellings, measuring up to 40 x 18 feet, in the eastern counties most affected by the 1381 revolt. However, he suggests that the cottages of the poorer peasantry were likely, on average, to have been smaller than those in the open-field regions of central and southern England. But, regardless of their size, peasant houses were seldom hovels and were constructed to last, as is evident from the survival today of many fourteenth century dwellings. Typical building materials included oak or ash timber posts, nails, wattle and daub for infilling the walls, and thatch for the roofs.[3] Tenants were expected to take care of these buildings, and were fined for 'waste' if they allowed them to deteriorate. Beyond the family messuage, the household would have had its own 'toft', an enclosed plot of land used either for the cultivation of subsistence crops such as peas or beans, or as pasture for a handful of sheep or pigs. Whereas the toft or close was a private parcel of land cultivated by the individual household, the vast majority of farming activity was communal. Arable land was generally farmed by teams of neighbours, who shared their labour, their ploughs and their oxen. In much of England a typical household cultivated a 'yardland' or half a yardland (or, if poorer, a fraction of a yardland), comprising non-contiguous strips distributed around the open fields. These yardlands were grouped into 'hides' – the unit for which a group of neighbours and their plough were responsible. Although measurements were not always uniform, a typical yardland was thirty acres, and four were usually aggregated to make a 'hide' of one-hundred and twenty acres. Together the households supplied the oxen to propel the plough for their 'hide' - although as long ago as 1941 Homans cautioned against imposing a neat schema on what may well have been a more chaotic reality.[4] It is worth noting than in Essex and East Anglia the standard arable holdings were much smaller, closer to five acres per household, and that in this region co-operative farming did not always function along the classical lines described above.[5] At the very bottom of rural society were the cotters who, unlike the yardlanders, did not have a stake in the common fields and pasture, but instead eked out a very marginal subsistence from whatever they could generate from the plots attached to their dwellings.

Perhaps the best-known social feature of the medieval countryside was the division between free and un-free tenants. Although described generically as serfdom, the condition of the un-free was known at the time by the legal term of villeinage. Like so many other features of the rural economy, villeinage had long predated the arrival of the Normans, but it dove-tailed well with their system of agriculture which was based on the 'manor'. (The manor was the property of a lord, whether a dynasty or a corporation such as a church or abbey, and, in its simplest form, comprised all of the fields, pasture, meadows, woodlands, ponds and buildings within its bounds. Some manors had the lord living on site in a principal residence, but many - especially those owned by corporations and other major proprietors - did not.) One of the peculiarities of the medieval village was that free tenants and villeins often lived side by side, and frequently there was no discernible difference in their living standards. The status of villeinage was often attached to the tenancy of a particular holding and so, bizarrely, a free man could have a second identity as a villein for one of the pieces of land that he held. A royal inquisition of 1279-80 showed that while less than one third of the free tenants assessed enjoyed holdings of either a half or a whole yardland, the figure was doubled for the villeins. Although the vast majority of the very smallest holdings were in the hands of villeins, and the very largest in those of free men, those in the middle of the range were more likely to be subject to un-free tenure.[6] Moreover, the distribution of villein land tenures was far from even across the kingdom. In the areas formerly under The Danelaw, extending from Northamptonshire up to Yorkshire, villeins barely formed the majority of peasants, while in Kent the practice was non-existent, due to the endurance of an ancient form of local free tenure called 'gravelkind'.[7] However, in other areas, such as East Sussex, villeinage was highly prevalent.[8]

Before considering the daily realities of villeinage, it is necessary to establish its legal foundations. Villeinage was upheld by the Common Law, and the royal courts were prepared to enforce the rights of land holders who could prove their claims at trial. The law did not seek to define the customs of individual manors or estates on questions such as rents and labour services, but rather was concerned with broader questions such as the status of the villein vis-à-vis his tenancy, his family and the other laws of the realm.

The legality of villeinage rested on a few basic assumptions, the most important being that the villein and his immediate family were chattels of the lord, and could thus be bought and sold. This also meant that a villein had no title to his property, although in actual fact even the poorest serfs did possess household animals, furnishings and implements necessary for their own subsistence. Significantly, a villein was not held to be financially responsible and so, like a child, was not liable for debt. Unsurprisingly, it was not unheard of for debtors to claim to be villeins. Also, the villein was tied to the land, and could not quit his tenancy without the permission of his lord. But the lord himself was under an obliga-tion not to maltreat his villeins to the extent that they fled his lands, as he would then be guilty of committing an offence of waste.[9]

Although tied to the land, the villein had no personal estate in his tenancy, including the right of inheritance. In strict legal terms the lord was always the villein's heir, but in actual fact hereditary succession ensured a continuity of cultivation, and so it effectively became the norm. Two customs in particular were central features of villein tenures. The 'heriot' was a customary payment owed by the villein's heir on his death, and it often took the form of the best beast owned by the household. Villeins also had no freedom when it came to the marriage of their children, and relied upon the acquiescence of their lord in all major family arrangements. Consequently a 'merchet' was payable to the lord when the daughter of a villein married.

Ultimately, it was the villein's relationship to the Common Law that distinguished him or her from a free tenant. Whereas a free tenant could bring a civil action against his lord in the court of Common Pleas, this avenue was entirely barred to the villein, who was even ineligible to serve as a witness or a juror. But the villein was included within the scope of the criminal law, and could be tried before the King's Bench for trespasses and felonies (the latter including capital offences such as murder, rape and robbery). A villein could appeal (i.e. accuse) his lord of felonies, although this right was confined to the crimes of sedition, treason, maiming and attempted homicide.[10]

One of the great iniquities of villeinage was the power of the manor court to regulate the life of the villein and those of his dependants. Whereas the free tenant could seek a remedy in the civil law, the villein was limited to his own lord's court. Given that his pleading was more than likely to collide directly with the interests of his lord, the unfairness (and occasional absurdity) of this system is manifest. The strict legal division between free and villein tenants was maintained in the functioning of the manor court, which assumed separate identities as 'the court baron' and 'the customary court' when hearing their respective pleas.[11] Presided over by the lord's steward, the 'customary court' was the first and last forum for the villein seeking redress. There was no appeal against its decisions.

The daily realities of villeinage depended entirely on the customs of the particular manor, and the demands made by the lord. Typically, the villein was subjected to a number of demands on his time and labour, reflecting the rhythms and cycles of the agricultural year, and the necessity of mobilising the resident population of the manor at certain key times. Whereas the free tenant was paid in cash for his labour, the villein received only payment in kind, usually in the form of food or raw commodities. Ploughing was one of the main obligations, and teams of ploughs, men and beasts were organised by the manor court. Harvest-time was perhaps the most labour-intensive period of the year, and while all the men were obliged to reap, women and children played their part in gathering and the provision of refreshments for the workers in the fields. The mowing of hay from the meadows in the manor was another collective obligation for the tenants of the manor. By the thirteenth century elaborate customs had developed surrounding the lord's obligation to provide bread, ale and other victuals to the reapers, and this practice may be linked to the festivities that later grew up around the completion of the harvest. Other obligations on villein tenants included the carriage or driving of commodities and stock to the market, and the haulage of building materials. For the lord the expenses of building and repair could be defrayed considerably through the use of villeins who owed a certain number of days of haulage every year.[12] Some of the heaviest customary demands were made on ecclesiastical estates, such as the bishop of Ely's manor of Walpole (Norfolk), where the tenants were obliged to labour for the lord six days a week.[13] However, by the fourteenth century many lords were allowing their tenants to buy-out their labour dues, and make cash payments by way of commutation. In 1345–6 the records of the earl of Warwick's Worcestershire manor of Elmley Castle record the commutation of more than 4,000 individual works owed by the tenants.[14]

Given the considerable disadvantages of villein tenure, the status of individuals was contested by lords and tenants alike. Proprietors were concerned to uphold their rights over villeins, and were particularly concerned by those who either vacated their holdings or contested their status. In the event of recalcitrance on the part of the tenant, the lord could move a writ in the county court, instructing the sheriff to seize the alleged villein and produce him or her for the examination of their status. If the individual claimed to be free, the case would be put before a jury in the county court, with the onus upon the lord to prove the alleged villein's un-free status. Any failure of proof on the part of the lord would result in an automatic verdict of free status for the alleged villein. Equally, if the alleged villein failed to appear to plead his case, then he would forfeit his free status regardless of any other evidence. In order to determine the case, the court could produce the relatives of the alleged villein, and their status could have a decisive impact on the eventual verdict.[15] An example of a successful defence against a writ came in 1354, when Peter Redworth, a smith, was indicted on 10 January before the justices of the palatinate of Durham as an alleged villein of Bishop Thomas Hatfield. His assertion of free-status was put before the county's jurors, who accepted that his ancestors had been free since time immemorial, and he was discharged on 27 January.[16] One cast-iron proof of free status in the south of the kingdom was birth in the county of Kent, although this had to be proven. By the middle of the fourteenth century there was considerable unease among landholders about villeins contesting their status. In 1347, before the Black Death had revolutionised the condition of villeins, the case of a man claimed as a villein by the bishop of Ely went as far Parliament.[17] The whole question of villeinage would become even more divisive in the second half of the century.

ECONOMIC TRENDS BEFORE THE BLACK DEATH

For all of the growth and expansion associated with the economy of pre-Black Death England, there were a number of long-term trends pointing towards impending crisis in the rural economy and society. In the period 1315–17 violent climatic change inflicted such damage on arable crops that food production fell well short of the demands of a growing population. The ensuing famine showed the fragility of the subsistence equilibrium in the fourteenth-century countryside, and the disastrous consequences arising from its disturbance. Zvi Razi's examination of the Worcestershire manor of Halesowen showed that its population of adult males fell by fifteen per cent between 1315 and 1321, after a growth of forty per cent between 1271 and 1311. The chronicler Thomas Walsingham claimed that the poor were reduced to eating the remains of diseased animals.[18]

The relationship between the extent and productivity of arable cultivation, and the population trends of the late thirteenth and early fourteenth centuries, was an underlying weakness in the rural economy. At the time of the Conquest of 1066, the population of England had lain in the range 1.75–2.25 million, by recent estimates. A major expansion of the English economy occurred in the following two and a half centuries, coinciding with, and in some respects causing, a consistent growth in population. John Hatcher has suggested that at the turn of the fourteenth century England's population had peaked somewhere near the top of the 5–6 million range.[19]

The very real impact of this population growth upon daily life can be gathered from the evidence for Halesowen.[20] In the years of severest dearth, the poorest families would often die from starvation, thereby enabling their wealthier neighbours to extend into the vacated tenancies. Thus, periods of dearth and poor harvests accentuated the divisions between wealthier and poorer village families, which were well-established before the advent of the Black Death.

Although there was undoubtedly fierce competition among tenants for existing tenancies, landlords undertook major projects to expand the overall quantities of arable land under cultivation, in order to feed the growing population. This expansion was achieved through a combination of the conversion of pasture to tilled soil, and the 'assarting' (clearing and ploughing) of woodland, waste and upland scrub. However, the reliance upon such land to fill the potential deficit of food supply and demand brought its own difficulties. One of the principal challenges was the maintenance of soil fertility. Many areas of the West Midlands practised a two-fold rotation, in which sheep grazed, and manured, the arable land. However, this system easily fell prey to soil exhaustion. The vulnerability of sheep to murrain, scab, and other infections often compromised rotation, while the lack of 'slack in the system' meant that bad weather and poor harvests could easily disrupt the cycles of cultivation.

Where arable could not be 'assarted', holdings would be sub-divided to accommodate the families of tenants. Perhaps the most obvious signs of land-hunger can be discerned in the buoyant rents and entry fines charged on holdings. On some estates held by lay and ecclesiastical magnates in the southern counties, entry fines exceeded £2, and the ceiling was pushed as high as £5 for entry to a large holding of more than one yardland. Hilton has shown that, on Lord Berkeley's manors in Gloucestershire, entry fines and other profits of court helped to cushion the lord's income. By the turn of the fourteenth century, these fines almost equalled the net yield of rent, and thus constituted almost half of the Berkeley manors' annual worth to their lord.[21] The use of manor courts to maximise profit through the exploitation of seigniorial rights was even more pronounced on the marcher lordships of Wales. Although Wales did not experience unrest in 1381, the long-term pressure of seigniorial exploitation, and naked greed, created a climate of popular resentment that was highly receptive to the call of Owain Glyn Dwr, almost twenty years later.[22]

The inflation of annual cash rentals is no less striking than that of entry fines and other manorial court profits. Although no meaningful average figure can be given for rent increases at the turn of the fourteenth century, due to the very great disparities in fertility and size of holding between different regions, some individual examples can nevertheless be offered to illustrate the general trend. In mid-thirteenth-century Norfolk, some tenants who had been newly admitted to holdings were being charged 6d per acre, whereas those who were already established were paying only 4d. Clearly, lords had little difficulty in recovering the costs of assarting new arable lands. In parts of Sussex, the traditional 1d per acre charged on the Canterbury diocesan estates had doubled by the end of the thirteenth century.[23]

So far it has been shown how the population increases of the late thirteenth and early fourteenth centuries put the peasant population at a disadvantage, as the competition for tenancies enabled landlords to maximise incomes, entry fines and customary dues. However, this does not fully account for the economic depression of the peasantry, and their exclusion from the benefits of the expanding agrarian economy. In order to see the full picture, we need to comprehend the shifting ratio of wages to prices, and its impact upon peasant living standards, in the period 1250–c.1320.

One of the principal consequences of the land-hunger of this period was that peasants were compelled to augment their incomes through employment other than on their own holdings. However, the same forces that were inflating rents and entry fines were having a correspondingly depressant effect on wages. Given the ease with which lords could draw upon the population resident on their demesne lands, there was only a limited demand for casual, externally sourced labour at this time.

The long-term decline in peasants' earning capacity can best be illustrated by an examination of the wages paid by one of the more prominent ecclesiastical proprietors in the later middle ages.

Although we should note that religious corporations were among the most conservative and cost-conscious employers, their practices are all the more relevant to this story as they were prime targets for popular violence in 1381. On the manor of Hinderclay (Suffolk) Westminster Abbey had raised its wage rates by only 5% in the period 1270–1320, whereas prices for basic commodities had risen by twenty-five per cent.[24] These real-term reductions in wages are likely to have been replicated, to varying degrees, across the rural economy. Paradoxically, the famine of 1315–17 did permit a slight reversal of this trend, as the struggle to boost arable production in the 1320s did increase the demand for labour. However, the overall picture is one of wages failing to keep pace with the costs of living over the longer term. By the early 1300s it had become cheaper for many lords to pay casual labourers fully in cash, than to offer them a supplementary food ration.

The movement of commodity prices in this period was also broadly to the disadvantage of peasants. Although individual peasant households did have a small stake in the commercial economy through the sale of surplus crops, and the retail of ale and foodstuffs, they were also consumers, and their lack of liquidity often rendered them very vulnerable to price fluctuations.

Generally, prices in the English economy had been subject to a fairly consistent inflationary trend from the second half of the twelfth century through to the second decade of the fourteenth century. Two reasons for this suggested by Hatcher and Miller are: increasing importation of bullion due to buoyant exports, and the stagnation in the costs of labour, which has already been noted. In addition the general growth of trade within England in this period may have stimulated demand for commodities. It would seem that this general pattern of growth in the rural economy was sustained into the first quarter of the fourteenth century.[25] However, the broad trend of rising prices in fourteenth-century England masks dramatic fluctuations caused by short-term phenomena such as poor weather and livestock epidemics. One of the most unstable decades was that from 1310 to 1320, which included the famine of 1315–17, during which the price of a quarter of wheat rose from just under 6s to 8s. For poorer peasant families who were reliant on the purchase of food, such periods of dearth could tip the balance from a marginal existence to outright starvation.

However, a large proportion of the rural population was able to find much of its sustenance from home-grown produce. This generally consisted of garden produce such as onions, leeks and cabbages. Those peasants able to rear ewes augmented their diet with dairy products, and the inventories left by more prosperous families contain pails and other utensils necessary for cheese production. Something of the wealthier peasant's diet is apparent from the description of Chaucer's *Franklin*:

> *An householdere, and that a greet, was he:*
> *Seint Julian he was in his countree.*
> *His breed, his ale, was always after oon;*
> *A bettre envyned man was nowher noon.*
> *Withoute bake mete was nevere his hous,*
> *Of fishe and flessh, and that so plentevous*
> *It snewed in his hous of mete and drynke;*
> *Of all deyntees that men koude thynke,*
> *After the sondry sesons of the yeer,*
> *So chaunged he his mete and his soper.*

Contrastingly, the poorer or landless peasant may have depended upon a ration from his master for much of his sustenance. Dyer has calculated that an annual allowance of twelve bushels was sufficient to produce 1½ lbs of bread daily, which constituted about a half of the minimum calorific intake necessary to sustain a labourer.[26]

Another supplement to the peasant diet could be found in hunting and trapping. However, livestock and game were heavily protected throughout the middle ages, and even the king's tenants-in-chief required a charter to enjoy free-warren, or the hunting of smaller game on their lands. Game rights in fourteenth-century England offered the most dramatic illustration of the horizontal tiers of hierarchy. Deer and boar were the exclusive preserve of the crown and the nobility, and their well protected parks and chases were policed strenuously. Indeed, the penalties for felling royal or private forests, let alone the poaching of game, were severe and readily enforced. The demands of the religious calendar ensured the popularity of fish in noble households, and the stocking of private ponds was very common. Swans were highly prized, both for their consumption (flesh as well as eggs) and as status symbols. Even rabbits were farmed in artificially constructed warrens for the noble household and the market – a telling sign of the 'privatisation' of nature on noble estates. Only the songbirds were left for the poor man with his nets. However, the judicial records of the fourteenth century make clear that the peasantry did not always confine their hunting within the licit bounds. In addition to the ubiquitous taking of rabbits, and hares for the cooking pot, poaching of more valuable game was also carried out by organised criminal gangs. On one night alone in 1356 the Earl of Arundel lost more than 100 swans from his ponds at Arundel Castle.[27]

Although the medieval peasantry were surrounded by animals, their diet was predominantly vegetable and cereal-based, and augmented with eggs and cheese. Some households had gardens which supported leeks and onions, while orchards were highly prized. The single most frequently prepared meal is likely to have been a form of pottage prepared from oats, peas or beans, depending on the season and the regional variations of arable crops. Many villeins received an allocation of wheat, which they were obliged to grind in the lord's mill. Christoper Dyer has calculated that a typical allowance of wheat would have yielded a peasant sufficient flour to produce somewhere between 1¼ and 1½ lbs of bread per day. Malt allowances were also common, which enabled many peasants to brew their own ale and retail the surplus to their neighbours. The retail of milk and cheese was also fairly common, although Dyer's discovery of cooked eel pasties for sale in four-teenth century Lakenheath (Suffolk) stands out as highly unusual.[28]

Peasant households certainly kept pigs and hens for their own consumption, but many families would have lived for months without tasting meat – which was usually reserved for a special occasion. This contrasts strongly with the patterns of consumption of the noble household. A servant resident in the earl of Warwick's household in 1420 would have sat down to more than 2lbs of meat per day, in the form of mutton, lamb, poultry and game, as well as a bread and ale allowance.[29]

What generalisations can be made about rural society on the eve of the plague's arrival in 1348? Perhaps the most obvious conclusion to be drawn was that the economic trends of the decades prior to the Black Death had accentuated the disparities of wealth and economic activity within rural society. Although some wealthier peasants had been able to capitalise on the drive to 'assart' new arable lands, the balance of economic advantage lay firmly with the proprietors, their agents and officials, and the middlemen of the rural economy. It is no coincidence that one of the characters satirised in *The Canterbury Tales* was the Miller, whose occupation had long been a byword for sharp practice and corruption.

The divisions within rural society and the tenuous hold on subsistence endured by the poorest were most clearly shown by a series of disasters that appeared almost as a prologue to the arrival of plague. The death of Edward I heralded not only the succession of a disastrous king, but also that of terrible years of dearth in the countryside, following an abnormally pronounced swing from heavy precipitation (1310–14) to drought (1321–4). As Bolton has noted, the rapid population growth of the previous decade had pushed to the limits the capacity of producers to satisfy the demands for food, with the result that there was no 'slack in the system'. By the summer of 1316, the price of a quarter of wheat had increased by three-hundred and twenty-five per cent on the previous year. Moreover, the arable disasters of 1315–17 were complemented by an outbreak of murrain that destroyed upwards of twenty-five per cent and, in extreme cases, fifty per cent, of some sheep flocks. To complete the litany of agricultural disaster, rinderpest broke out in 1319–21, devastating herds and creating a severe shortage of draught animals. Ominously, the harvest failures of 1315–16 were followed by an enteric epidemic, which may have claimed as many as ten per cent of the population.[30]

During the reign of Edward I the crown's policies of military expansionism had begun to impinge increasingly upon the lives of the peasantry. As if the disasters of weather, famine, and human and animal epidemic were not enough, the first three Edwards were increasingly concerned to pass on the costs of their wars to their poorer subjects. The broadening of the tax base had begun in earnest in the 1290s, with the outbreak of war with France (1294) and Scotland (1296). The disaster of Bannockburn in 1314 – coinciding unhappily with the famine period – prompted the government of Edward II to levy two particularly heavy subsidies in 1315 and 1316. Although Maddicott has shown that the impact of this taxation varied broadly according to local factors such as the zeal or caprice of the collectors, there was nevertheless an inbuilt inequity in a system that assessed moveable goods alone, and exempted landed income. For those who had to sell their seed-corn or implements, the tax would have bitten deep.[31]

In the last years before the advent of the Black Death in England, landlords began to experience some of the economic pressure that their tenants had endured for decades. By the second quarter of the century, the rural economy was in a profound recession, with a serious contraction in landed incomes.

The purpose of the first half of this chapter has been to demonstrate that, although defined by overall trends of growth in population and trade, both domestic and overseas, the rural economy of England prior to the Black Death was subject to intense strains and pressures. Land-hunger, price fluctuation and low wages ensured that those at the bottom of society were highly vulnerable to economic reversals. When we come to consider the economic and social causes of the 1381 revolt, we need to understand that the English peasantry had endured almost a century of instability in its living standards, and an existence that was, at best, precarious, and, at worst, verging on starvation.

EPIDEMIC AND POPULATION CHANGE, *c.*1349–1377

The arrival of the Black Death in the south of England in the summer of 1348 brought about a phase of dramatic change in the English countryside. Above all, the radical decrease in England's population, estimated most recently in the 47–48% range, had a major impact on wages, prices and standards of living throughout England.[32] The responses of the crown, the law courts and land-holders to the medium-term effects of the Black Death would play a major role in creating an environment of despair, resentment and frustrated expectations among the English commons.

In the short-term, the devastating incidence of plague-related mortality brought to a halt much of the economic activity in the English countryside. Sudden falls in production and the abandon-ment of peasant holdings were the most immediate consequences. In the Oxfordshire village of Cuxham, all of the twelve villeins who were alive at the beginning of 1349 were dead by the end of the year.

Many settlements lost such a high proportion of their popula-tion that there were not enough resident labourers to sustain minimum levels of cultivation. Consequently, the great arable expansion of the past two and half centuries was thrown into a dramatic reverse. Farming was pinched both by the inability to maintain production due to mortality in the work-force, and the consequent lack of demand for cereal foods from the declining population as a whole.[33] There can be little doubt that the years immediately following the advent of plague were bleak ones indeed for the landholders.

However, the peasants who survived the terrible mortality of 1349 found themselves in a world where the equation of supply and demand had been turned upside down. Contemporary estate records show that, within weeks or months of the Black Death's arrival, the peasants themselves were well aware of the changed economic realities. As Horrox has shown in the case of the men of Rudheath in Cheshire, who threatened to quit the manor unless their rent was rebated by one-third, tenants used their newly found economic leverage to considerable effect.[34] Towns sustained a serious downturn in all forms of economic activity – and in many cases there was no detectable recovery until the mid-Tudor period. Contraction in the supply of commodities for sale caused a slump in market activity. Market stalls, like agricultural tenancies, frequently stood empty.[35]

For landlords, the most noticeable, and painful, consequence of the epidemic was the keen awareness among labourers of their own rising value. Henry Knighton, the cellarer of Leicester Abbey, recorded with horror the sudden escalation in wage demands that his own house faced: 'In the following autumn (1350) no one could get a reaper for less than 8d with food, a mower for less than 12d with food'. In facing doubled wage demands, Leicester Abbey was far from unrepresentative of both lay and ecclesiastical lords.

Although the plague was socially undiscriminating in its choice of victims, universal feelings of horror at its impact did not translate into a common endeavour towards its resistance, and nor did it forge any sense of unity through adversity. Partially, this may be accounted for by a certain religious fatalism in the face of what was widely perceived as divine punishment for the evils of the age. But, among the poorer landholding classes, like the Tory squirearchy in the age of the Corn Laws, there was a visceral fear that they had the most to lose from these apparently uncontrollable movements in the rural economy. Within months of the advent of the plague, the more modest landholders were articulating both their fears of impoverishment arising from the wage demands of their inferiors, and their resentment against those more able to absorb these crippling pressures.

However, unlike the starving peasants of 1315–17, the knights and gentlemen had a formal apparatus to express the pain that they felt in their receivers' rolls. Representation in Parliament gave the knights and esquires a place at the fulcrum of the political community, and at the confluence of royal fiscal need and the representation of property. One of the consequences of the military ambitions of the first three Edwards had been the increasing need to secure the consent of property-holders to tax their wealth. The participation of the knights, gentry and townsmen had become a regular feature of Parliament since the 1290s, and they had already found a voice in criticising Edward III's highly unpopular wool tax experiments of the late 1330s and early 1340s.[36]

On 18 June 1349, pressure from the Parliamentary Commons bore fruit in the promulgation of the Ordinance of Labourers, the first phase of a statutory wages policy which would become one of the most contentious collections of legislation in the history of Parliament. In the words of R.C. Palmer: 'The legislative response to the plague was relatively immediate and based more on impressions, suspicions and expectations, all undoubtedly mixing both truth and exaggeration – than any other major medieval enactments'.[37] The entire tone of the Ordinance was one of reproach towards labourers and artisans seeking to gain a competitive wage for their labour.

Both the Ordinance and the Statute were underpinned by coercion. Work became compulsory for all male and female labourers and craftsmen who were physically fit and under the age of sixty – and alms were to be withheld from those who were deemed to be shirking. Quite simply, the English crown wanted to turn the clock back to 1348, and compel employers to offer, and labourers to accept, the wage levels of that year. Furthermore, the Statute also sought to clamp down on the physical mobility of labour, as taking to the road in search of better conditions had become common practice. The testimony of two men before local officials could secure conviction and imprisonment of those refusing to accept work according to the official terms and conditions.

Although principally directed at labourers and artisans, the Statute was also aimed at those employers who colluded in wage inflation at the expense of those of their rivals less able to offer competitive rates. Those who employed a labourer or servant who had absconded before the end of a term of employment were liable to imprisonment, while the offering of excessive wages was punishable by fines.

The Ordinance and Statute also sought to tackle the inflation in the prices of services and commodities. All of the more common crafts were included, such as saddlers, skinners, tailors, smiths, carpenters, masons, tilers and all forms of carriers. Retailers, including butchers, poulterers, fishmongers, bakers and brewers were subject to similar restrictions.[38] The following decades would witness a profound conflict between two contrasting paradigms – that of free-floating wages and prices in the 'black' economy, versus the statutory restrictions enacted and upheld by the crown.[39]

Recently, Anthony Musson has drawn attention to the local restrictions on wages and mobility, which existed before the Ordinance and Statute. It is possible that these local measures were in the forefront of the minds of the Parliamentary Commons during the formulation of the Ordinance and Statute. Moreover, the machinery for the enforcement for local measures controlling prices and labour was readily adaptable to the new royal legislation. The co-operation of constables, bailiffs and borough courts was necessary for the enforcement of the new laws in the localities. It is clear that our understanding of the genesis of royal legislation and its application must take account of these earlier local templates, which highlight the fact that, although distinctive in its scope and the severity of its punishments, the Statute of Labourers represented the culmination of a number of restrictions on the daily lives of the poorer commons.[40]

What truly distinguished the Statute of Labourers was the determination underpinning its enforcement, and the totality of its reach into the lives of the king's subjects. The first commission of enforcement ran from 18 June 1349, the day of the Ordinance's promulgation. In the first decade of enforcement 671 justices were employed, many of whom were already serving on the commissions of the peace – the principal agency of law enforcement in the English countryside. Although there has been debate over the effectiveness of the statute, there can be little doubt that its enforcement impinged upon the lives of thousands of labourers and employers.

Although the justices originally sat specifically for the purpose of trying cases under the Statute, by the 1360s they had become effectively integrated within the commissions of the peace. The fact that enforcement had become subsumed into the local structures of power, where the ranks of the justices of the peace were dominated by the leading landholders of the county, is likely to have accentuated the sense of alienation among those indicted under the Statute. Moreover, the justices' reliance on the testimony of local royal and seigniorial officials, such as bailiffs, reeves, constables and stewards paved the way for collusion, concealment and malicious prosecution. There can be little doubt that beneath the veneer of official records, there was widespread favouritism and score-settling. Puttnam showed that within months of the enactment of the Statute in 1351, Edmund Northtoft, one of the justices of labourers in Essex, was indicted and convicted before the King's Bench for the extortion of payments from men of various occupations, under pain of unlawful imprisonment. One of the most extreme examples of a landowner merging his private economic interests with devolved judicial authority was Lionel Bradenham, the dominant proprietor in the Essex village of Langenhoe. His repeated extortion of unjust fines, which he collected with the assistance of an armed gang, caused the nearby town of Colchester to petition, successfully, for his dismissal as a JP in 1362.[41] The reality of heavy-handedness and corruption in the processes of enforcement may have lingered long in the memories of those who felt that they had suffered at the hands of the commissioners. We must remember the cumulative impact of years of royal intrusion on the daily lives of the commons when considering reactions to the Poll Tax collectors in 1377–80.

There is also evidence for community solidarity in the face of the demands of the commissioners. Henry Green, a justice of labourers for Northamptonshire, produced his own duplicates of assessed fines to show that the local collectors had either failed to impose the fines, or embezzled their proceeds.

Although some historians have expressed doubts about the effectiveness of the Statute, it is nonetheless true that the processes of indictment and conviction were very real for transgressors brought before the commissioners. In many instances cases were heard in batches, so that entire teams of men and women engaged in seasonal labour or cottage industry could be fined for receipt of excessive wages. Typical of this was the judicial session in the Herefordshire village of Bodenham in 1357, when about forty male and female textile workers were fined for various infractions against the 1351 statute.[42] Although there may have been a vaguely ritualised and mutually accepting element to these exercises, they perpetuated the conflictual dynamic between the crown and the people that had first crystallised during Edward I's fiscal impositions of the 1290s.

The kingdom-wide enforcement of the Statute of Labourers raised the stakes for those seeking to better themselves through improved wages. In addition to escaping from their lords and masters, the errant labourers now had to evade the attentions of commissioners, and those keen to traduce them to the authorities. Around 1375–80, Thomas St John, lord of the manor of Glympton, (Oxon.) wrote to his near neighbour Sir Philip la Vache, steward of the royal estate at Woodstock (on the site of the present Blenheim Palace):

> To my dearest master, Sir Philip la Vache, keeper of the manor of Woodstock, Thomas St John petitions that one Thomas Hawkins, villein of the said Thomas, pertaining to the manor of Glympton, is residing in Wooton, within the demesne of my lord the King at Woodstock, and may it please my lord to ordain that Thomas St John should have the said villein as law and reason demands, for right and in the service of charity.[43]

Thomas Hawkins' escape from a small landlord in the hope of better wages on the crown estate must have been replicated many hundreds of times in the decades between 1349 and 1381. Although Hawkins failed in his bid for economic emancipation, many cultivators, artisans and labourers were able to capitalise on the changed economic conditions of the second half of the fourteenth century. In what ways did the survivors exploit their new circumstances, and what were the broader economic and social consequences?

One of the most distinctive transformations wrought upon the rural economy by the Black Death, and the changed economic conditions that it brought, was the change from customary to lease-hold tenure. For centuries peasants had held their dwellings and plots of land according to the customs of their particular manor. As we have seen, some manors levied heavy entry fines and labour services, while the tenants were vulnerable to highly arbitrary rent increases. In addition to seeking higher wages, the post-plague peasantry exploited their new-found bargaining power to secure various forms of written tenancy. This enabled them to bargain over conditions such as the duration of the lease, as well as the payment of a fixed rent that was increasingly (but far from exclusively) rendered in cash. One such form of written tenure was the 'copyhold', so called because the terms of the tenancy were copied on the manorial court roll. The emergence of the written lease not only gave the tenants greater security and stability of occupancy, it was also an indelible affirmation of their rising social and economic expectations.

The rise of the copyhold and other forms of written lease did not entail the death of customary tenure. Rather, the majority of peasant holdings in England continued to be held by custom, but the terms of these customs were changing dramatically. Often substantial yeomen and gentlemen would enter into customary tenancies, for which cash rent would be their sole liability. On some later four-teenth-century estates the actual terms and conditions of copyhold and customary tenures differed very little in reality. Customary tenants could even avoid the payment of a heriot – which, hitherto, had been almost a defining characteristic of this tenurial model.[44]

In the face of declining profits, many late fourteenth-century landlords abandoned demesne cultivation and farmed out parcels of land, or entire manors, to a contractor, who would pay a set farm. Some peasant families who, in the previous generation, had held tenancies on the most disadvantageous conditions, were now blending their own cultivation with the farming of former demesne lands.

In the decades following the Black Death the early beginnings of a peasant land market can be discerned, although it was not until the later fifteenth and early sixteenth centuries that it would attain the critical mass that finally dissolved the bonds of manorial control. In some areas, especially those where ecclesiastical lords and corporations predominated, there is very little evidence of a land-market, due to the permanence of their control.[45] But, in the counties surrounding London, where the feudal units of tenure had long been fragmented through sub-infeudations and sales, a primitive land-market was thriving. As the wealthier peasants accumulated more property, they began to emulate the nobility and gentry by making more elaborate provisions for its disposal and transmission. Alan McFarlane has drawn attention to the phenomenon of peasants disinheriting one son (on occasions the eldest, and thus the principal heir) for the benefit of another.[46]

Faced with the disintegration and fragmentation of the tradi-tional units of feudal tenure, landholders made strenuous efforts to reverse trends that they considered to be only to their disadvantage. One of the most forceful, and best documented, campaigns to restore seigniorial power was waged on the estates of the palatinate of Durham. Like many corporate lords, the diocese of Durham benefited from compact estates, professional management, well-kept records and an institutional permanence that insulated it from the frailties of dynastic discontinuity. Armed with all of these advantages, Bishop Thomas Hatfield bullied and coerced his tenants to an unprecedented degree, and was not averse to imprisoning those who were rumoured to be planning to abscond from their manors. His 'halmote', or episcopal court, was particularly assiduous in compelling individuals, and entire communities, to perform all of their traditional customary dues. Something of the maximalist tone of Hatfield's administration can be gathered from the prosecution of the villagers of Cassop in 1358 for not farming the lands of a tenant while he served in the royal army in Scotland.

However, the very fact that Bishop Hatfield resorted to such extreme measures has a certain ring of desperation. Moreover, when some of his tenants called his bluff by refusing to accept tenancies with rents higher than the existing 1d per acre, he had to back down, lest his lands went unfarmed and reverted to the waste from which the diocese had claimed them. Indeed, a sudden shift from conflict to collusion was apparent in 1355, when the Bishop allowed the men of Killerby to continue holding by 'Pennyfarm' providing that the concession be kept secret from his other tenants. Clearly, the 'seigniorial reaction' was not a sudden and decisive counter-blow, but a multitude of battles of will fought out in individual villages and manors, and determined by localised shifts in the scales of economic advantage between lords and tenants. Britnell's conclusion that the seigniorial reaction on the Durham estates yielded equivocal, and occasionally diminishing, returns, may hold good as a general summary of this period.[47]

Although the 'seigniorial reaction' in Durham, and elsewhere in England, was fought out largely through argument, passive resistance, and communal bloody-mindedness, the eschewal of violence was neither a given nor an absolute. Various factors could lead to violence, but one common paradigm was the collision of the irresistible force of peasant grievance with the immovable object of seigniorial intransigence. Although unique in its scale, geographical extent, and the degree of violent energy that it released, the 1381 revolt must also be seen in the context of previous acts of popular disturbance and protest.

POPULAR PROTEST AND RESISTANCE BEFORE 1381

As we have seen, the great majority of the people of England had no formal role in the polity. The tenure of freehold property remained the determining qualification for direct participation in the governance of the kingdom, with the result that the peasantry and poorer townsmen were no closer to enjoying a direct stake in governance. Similarly, the mechanisms of local justice were also far out of the reach of the peasantry. The offices of sheriff, justice of the peace, coroner and an escheator (responsible for the collection of the king's feudal income) were already becoming the preserve of the knights and squires. The merging of the office of justice of labourers (responsible for the enforcement of the 1351 statute) with that of justice of the peace was a telling statement of the close interconnection of the economic interests and judicial powers of the gentry. Other than their participation in the lesser offices of seigniorial administration, such as those of reeve, bailiff and forester, the peasants had virtually no stake in governance above the level of the manor court. The scope for direct contact between the peasantry and the crown was very limited. Peasants charged with serious crimes would appear before the justices of the King's Bench. When the King passed through the localities the commons were exposed to one of the most hated practices of royal governance – purveyance for the Household. Intended as a system for enabling the royal household to purchase victuals at a reserve price lower than their market value, purveyance was widely regarded as being little better than theft. Sometimes, those subject to purveyance were not paid at all, or were issued with tallies that could be redeemed for only a fraction of the value of the victuals that had been provided.

Therefore, the only regular peacetime interfaces between the crown and its poorer subjects were the mechanisms of taxation, purveyance and judicial control. It is, of course, true that the peasant might catch a glimpse of his king on the field of battle, but the glaring differentials in the survival prospects of the mounted classes, and the common foot soldiers, were hardly conducive to a sense of fellowship in arms.

The gradations between peasant non-compliance with manorial control and outright revolt were blurred and indistinct. Throughout the fourteenth century, individual acts of personal resistance, ranging from delinquency, neglect and unlicensed movement of labour, through to open defiance of lordship, are recorded on the court rolls of the landholders. Collective resistance was rarer but, in its infrequency, was all the more striking.

A direct challenge to seigniorial power came in Cheshire in 1336, when the men of Darnall and Over clashed with their lord, the Abbot of Vale Royal. The gist of their complaint was that the Abbot treated them as serfs, whereas they claimed that they had a royal charter confirming their status as freeholders. The Abbot's first response had been to imprison those protesting tenants until they swore that they would not resist his will again. However, once released they set out into the north-east of England to petition the King, who was then attending to the war with Scotland. Refused an audience, they resorted to robbery to sustain themselves, and were eventually brought before the royal justices, who had them incarcerated in Nottingham gaol under suspended sentence of death. On their release, they took their grievances to Parliament at Westminster, but to no effect. Frustrated by the failure of their efforts to obtain the King's lordship, they tried to intercept the Abbot on his homeward journey, at Exton in Rutland. In the ensuing confrontation, one of the Abbot's grooms was slain, and the Darnall men found themselves once again before the royal courts, at Stamford.

Perhaps a combination of the confused circumstances of the case, and the desire of the royal justices to get rid of the Darnall men as soon as possible, resulted in their release. Although avoiding the gallows, the men of Darnall had little to show for their extensive travels. As they were tenants of a royally founded house, in a royal palatinate, the writ they had obtained at Stamford commanding the restitution of their property was useless. The Abbot of Vale Royal compounded their humiliation by making them swear their villein status on the gospels, and stand as bare-headed penitents in the choir of the church, as conditions for the re-entry to their tenancies.[48]

Perhaps the overriding conclusion to be drawn from the Darnall rising was that an isolated and rurally based group, acting during a time of domestic political calm, could have no hope of success in the face of intransigence by a lord who enjoyed an overwhelming advantage of legal and financial resources, and the support of the crown. However, given a different set of variables in the power equation, the outcome of popular resistance could be very different.

The prelude to one of the longest lasting – and bitterly fought – disputes had a fairly innocuous beginning in 1314, when certain men of St Albans refused to grind their corn in the mills of their lord, Abbot Hugh Eversdone. In a test case, one of their number, Robert Lymsbury, was tried in the county court on charges of having assaulted the Abbot's bailiff and ejected him from his house, when he attempted to prevent the illicit use of a handmill. The exclusive right of the Abbey to mill corn was one of its most jealously guarded privileges. Convicted, Lymsbury was fined the substantial sum of 100s. Beneath the surface of this apparently insignificant brawl lurked a much larger question – were the people of St Albans burgesses of a town, or villeins of the Abbot's manor?

In 1326, as the reign of Edward II slid into civil war, the men of St Albans renewed their efforts to assert their independence. After a spate of attacks on the Abbey's property, and the erection of an improvised axe-guillotine in the town's market place, doubtless with the intention of focusing minds in the Abbey, the men of the town drew up a series of demands. Their main objective was to force the Abbey to recognise their burghal status. The men of St Albans were highly motivated and organised, as they had researched the privileges normally afforded to boroughs, and had retained serjeants-at-law to draw up their claims. They demanded representation in Parliament by two of their number elected from the town's franchise, the right of audience before the itinerant justices of the King's Bench, and the right to hold their own assizes of bread and ale. In addition, they also sought to strike at the Abbey's economic hegemony by claiming that the common lands, woods and fishponds of the town were vested corporately in the borough. Underpinning the entire manifesto was the assertion that St Albans' burghal status was confirmed by 'a certain book in the King's Treasury, which in English is called "Domesday"'. Abbot Hugh's dismissal of their claims resulted in a siege of the Abbey precinct, which was only halted by news that the crown had summoned the county levy to resist them. When Abbot Hugh suggested arbitration of the dispute at St Paul's London, the townsmen suspected that he was stalling on their demands, and resumed their attacks with renewed vigour. In the meantime, the townsmen's investment in legal counsel was yielding results, as on 8 February 1327 they secured royal writs addressing them as 'burgesses' and commanding the Abbey to desist from interfering in their liberties. A second writ instructed the inspection of the Hertfordshire volume of *Domesday*, in which St Albans was found to have had 'forty-six burgesses' in 1086. Under pressure from the crown, the St Albans case was committed to arbitration, in which it was concluded, on 10 March, that the town was a borough.

Although the Abbey bore its defeat with considerable ill-will, to the extent that Abbot Hugh was threatened with a mutiny from within his own house, the parties agreed to perambulate the boundaries of St Albans, in order to demarcate the Abbey precinct and the borough. Finally, on 16 March 1327, the men of St Albans drew up an indenture with the Abbey confirming their burghal status.[49] This, however, was not the end of the story, and we shall return to St Albans in 1381 to examine the dynamics of local protest within the broader context of the Great Rising.

One of the more striking features of the St Albans rising was the faith attached to the *Domesday Book* in the collective consciousness of the townsmen. There seemed to be no comparable popular attachment to any other royal records, and the potency of *Magna Carta* as a rallying cry for baronial discontent had faded by the middle of the fourteenth century. However, the talismanic power exerted by *Domesday* appeared to be increasing in the fourteenth century, and it became a central feature of the most significant popular movement before the 1381 revolt.

The best evidence for a common political attachment to the *Domesday Book* was uncovered by Rosamond Faith in her examination of a series of petitions submitted to the crown by forty villages in Wiltshire, Hampshire, Surrey, Sussex and Devon in 1377–8, which has become known as 'The Great Rumour'.[50] These petitions sought exemplifications of the entries relating to their villages in the *Domesday Book*, and endorsed with the Great Seal of England.

Faith has suggested that the petitioners were wanting to establish whether their communities had ever formed part of the royal demesne (i.e. the crown estate). In the collective consciousness of the English peasantry, the tenants of ancient demesne enjoyed a number of legal privileges, which they held to be perpetual and inalienable. The widespread currency of this belief is evident from Thomas Hawkins' decision to flee to Woodstock, a royal estate. The tenants of crown demesne, known as 'villein sokemen' did indeed enjoy a distinct status before the law. Villein sokemen were exempt from attendance at the hundred or county courts, and were also immune from a number of feudal dues. However, the extent of the ancient demesne had shrunk radically since 1066, and the majority of the petitioners were disappointed by the evidence from *Domesday*, as it failed to produce the evidence that they were seeking. The petitioners' faith in *Domesday* as an ineradicable record of their status as 'villein sokemen' demonstrated clearly their recognition of the power of the written word in shaping their lives. Evidently, the petitioners of 1377–8 were endowed with a collective sense of their tenurial and economic rights, and a willingness to jump through the necessary bureaucratic hoops to secure their confirmation.

By the beginning of the 1370s, the English countryside had experienced a series of violent changes that had transformed the conditions of rural existence. Although the advent of the Black Death in 1348 heralded the greatest changes to rural life prior to the enclosures of the eighteenth century, it must be seen in the context of a century of fluctuations in population, food production and living standards. Growth in the rural economy had peaked by *c.*1300, and the productive capacity of the arable sector was barely keeping up with the demands of a population that had increased dramatically over the past century. The fragility of this equilibrium of supply and demand in cereal production had become manifest during the famine years of 1315–17. Although those who survived the epidemic of 1348, and its subsequent visitations of the 1360s and 1370s, did enjoy improved conditions of labour and tenancy, this was only achieved in the face of the resistance of landholders. The responses of landlords varied greatly, some, such as Bishop Hatfield of Durham, fought a bitter struggle to maintain their feudal rights against the prevailing economic realities.

The economic disasters of the first half of the fourteenth century were compounded by the extension of the crown's fiscal reach to the wealth of its lesser subjects. From the late 1330s, the lay subsidy became the principal form of war finance for Edward III. Although England and France were at peace from 1360–9, the resumption of war in the 1370s heralded a renewal of the crown's fiscal demands on its subjects. But the military and diplomatic circumstances of the 1370s were very different from those of the 1340s and 1350s, when Edward III, the Black Prince and the other English war captains had delivered repeated, crushing victories. It is to this broader background of fiscal exhaustion and military defeat that the investigation of the causes of the 1381 revolt will now turn.

2

WAR AND PEACE: ENGLAND 1369–1381

A KINGDOM AT WAR

On the death of his grandfather, Edward III, in the third week of June 1377, Richard II succeeded to the throne of a kingdom at war. During the later phase of his reign, Richard II would strive to disentangle his kingdom from a war that he regarded as a *damnosa hereditas*. The reason for this wholesale rejection of his father and grandfather's policies can be found in the military and diplomatic catastrophes of the early years of his reign.

The high watermark of England's military fortunes had come in 1356, when the Black Prince had defeated and captured Jean II of France at Poitiers. However, in the following four years England had failed to press home this advantage. In the Treaty of Brétigny-Calais of 1360, Edward III had renounced his claim to the French crown, in return for tenure of the duchy of Aquitaine in full sovereignty. In the near decade of cold war that followed, Charles V had worsted England in every strategic and diplomatic gambit. In 1364 the new

French King secured the heiress of the county of Flanders for one of his sons, Philip, Duke of Burgundy. But the contest of the 1360s was won and lost in Spain, where England and France were backing rival candidates for the throne of Castile. From his base in Aquitaine, the Black Prince backed Pedro the Cruel, and in 1367 won a decisive victory at Najera against the rival Henry of Trastamara. But only two years later, Pedro was assassinated.[1] The major consequence of this was that France was able to draw upon the naval power of Castile to intercept English shipping and threaten the cross-channel wool trade. When hostilities resumed in 1369, France enjoyed a decisive advantage.[2]

The resumption of war in 1369 was the last thing that the English crown needed, as the diplomatic reversals it had sustained since 1360 meant that it had to adopt a reactive strategy from the outset. France's pretext for war in 1369 was the result of careful collusion with the leading native barons of Gascony, whose power flowed from the unpredictability of their loyalties. Their key grievance was the hearth-tax, known as the 'fouage', which the Black Prince had imposed on his principality of Aquitaine (granted to him by his father Edward III on 9 July 1362) on three successive occasions, in 1364, 1365 and again in 1366 (the danger of a sudden and repeated levying of heavy taxes would become all too clear during the reign of his son). Two of the most prominent Gascon barons, Arnaud Amanieu of Albret and Jean, count of Armagnac, contested the Prince's right to levy the fouage in their territories, which together comprised a large part of the principality. Their opposition was highly destabilising for English rule, and the French crown was quick to capitalise on their breakdown of relations with the Prince. Albret and Armagnac first appealed over the Prince's head to Edward III himself, but this may well have been a mere formality, as soon after they took their case to Charles V and to the French crown's supreme court, the *Parlement de Paris*. Armagnac was the first to lodge his appeal, in June 1368, but, once French royal approval was evident, many hundreds of Gascons followed his example over the following months. International knowledge of this royally encouraged flood of appeals was limited until December 1368, when Charles V pronounced that as king of France he was obliged to accept appeals from his Gascon vassals. By this time Charles V was well aware that war was imminent, and his armies were being readied for an offensive across the borders of Aquitaine. In January 1369 a French royal official, the seneschal of Toulouse, was sent into Aquitaine to deliver the summons to the Black Prince to attend the *Parlement de Paris*. Naturally, Prince Edward refused the summons and on 2 May of that year the *Parlement* pronounced him as contumacious. On 8 June Charles V publicly stated his intention of waging war against England. He was well aware of the panic that would arise in England as a result of his statement, but he also wished to prolong the uncertainty in the minds of his enemies, and so forbore from the ultimate step of declaring Aquitaine sequestrated until 30 November 1369, by which time his armies had already been in action for eleven months. England's desperation to avoid a war for which it was neither militarily nor financially ready was evident from the frantic diplomatic efforts that it made throughout 1368 and 1369.[3] Edward III and the Prince showed the weakness of their hand by offering to postpone the instalments of the ransom owed by France under the Bretigny treaty for the late Jean II (d.1364), while also hastily conceding additional French territorial demands.

But by this stage the French royal armies had already made disastrous inroads into the English-held lands. In the spring of 1369 the army of the duke of Anjou and Bertrand du Guesclin captured Rouergue, the Agenais and Perigord, territories which had been won at such cost by the English in the 1340s and 1350s. In the north of France, the county of Ponthieu, which had been guaranteed to Edward III in the 1360 treaty, fell to the French commander Hugues de Chatillon.[4] By the late spring of 1369 Edward III and his council were faced with the prospect of a collapse of English forces on both the northern and southern fronts.

A substantial army was sent to Aquitaine under the king's son Edmund, earl of Cambridge, and his son-in-law, John Hastings, earl of Pembroke, to reinforce Prince Edward and his great field commander, Sir John Chandos. With considerable forces at his disposal, including the veteran soldiers commanded by Chandos, Sir Robert Knolles and Sir Hugh Calveley, the Black Prince was able to maintain a credible defence of Aquitaine, the fighting at this time being characterised by the rapid capture, loss and re-capture of towns and castle.

But by the middle of summer 1369 a new threat emerged in the north of France, and one that threatened England directly. A large invasion force was being equipped at Harfleur under the command of Charles V's brother, Philip, duke of Burgundy.[5] To counter this threat John of Gaunt was sent to Calais in July 1369 at the head of an army of 5,000, which, with the assistance of 1,000 foreign mercenaries, recovered Ardres, Therouanne and St Pol over the following months.[6] However, a decisive victory would only have been possible through an engagement with the army of Philip of Burgundy, but neither commander took the initiative to attack when they met at Tournehem in Artois.[7] Later, in mid-September 1369, Burgundy retreated to St Omer and disbanded his forces. With the field open to him, Gaunt had the choices of either marching south-eastwards into the Isle de France and threatening Paris, or westwards into Normandy to attack Harfleur and St Omer, where the French were amassing their shipping. Choosing the latter option, Gaunt led his army into Normandy with the intention of attacking Harfleur. However, the defences of this great fortress were too much for his army, which may have lacked the specialist equipment for a major siege, and, after twelve days encamped outside its walls, he returned to Calais in mid-October. Although skirmishing continued under the forces of his lieutenants, Gaunt's expedition was effectively over and in December he returned to England.[8]

Although there may have been compelling tactical reasons underpinning his decisions, the inconclusive results of John of

Gaunt's 1369 expedition left him vulnerable to criticism. In fact, on this occasion he appeared to be far from negligent, keeping his army intact and harassing the French on their northern front, but it seems that he had already become something of a lightning conductor for English anxieties over the broader conduct of the war. An even worse year was to follow for the English, heralded by the loss on New Year's Eve of their greatest knight, Sir John Chandos, who was slain in a skirmish near St Salvin in Poitou.[9] In 1370 an expedition of 4,000 men set out from Winchilsea for Calais under the command of the experienced knight Robert Knolles. The route of his *chevauchee* took him towards Arras and into Vermandois, where he adopted the well-established tactic of burning and pillaging, to goad the French into offering battle, while also depriving them of resources and terrorizing the populace. After burning Pont-L'Evêque his army rode towards Paris, in whose environs he campaigned for some days, before striking south into Anjou. But, at Pont-Valin in Anjou, part of Knolles' army ran into the forces of du Guesclin, and the resulting defeat resulted in the break-up of the entire English expedition.[10]

Evidence of the fiscal strain imposed by expeditions of this sort is evident from the fact that only thirteen weeks of wages were guaranteed in the contracts that had been made with Knolles' men. If, as James Sherborne suggested, this had been intended as an economy (in the hope that the mercenary soldiers would live off the spoils of war), then it proved to a false one, as it may have contributed to the rapid collapse of Knolles' army after the defeat at Pont-Valin.[11]

England's woes were not confined to the course of the war on land. In April 1372 the earl of Pembroke was sent to Aquitaine as royal lieutenant with a brief to recruit a force of 3,000 local men to aid in its defence. His flotilla of about twenty ships set out from Plymouth in June, but on the 22nd of that month it was intercepted by a force of Castilian galleys off La Rochelle. Over the following day and a half Pembroke suffered a terrible defeat, losing all of his vessels to incendiary attacks, while the earl himself and his war chest of £12,000 fell into Castilian hands.[12] One of the knock-on effects of this defeat was the fall of La Rochelle to the French in September of that same year; a bitter blow to Edward III whose great relief expedition of 6,000 men was kept at Winchelsea by contrary winds.[13]

In the longer term the strategic costs of this defeat were measurable in more ways than merely the loss of resources and naval capability. The Franco-Castilian naval axis deprived England of its past dominance in the Channel, imperilling the transport of soldiers and supplies to Calais. Moreover, England's southern coastal towns were now more vulnerable to naval attack than at any time since the era of the Danish invasions. From the early 1370s a war which had hitherto been fought on French and Spanish soil came home to England, and public opinion, mediated through the members of the House of Commons who sat for the southern counties, became a real factor in the strategic equation.

One of the major consequences of the resumption of war in 1369 was a renewed search for allies on the part of Edward III. In the south England looked to Charles II of Navarre, whose Pyrenean kingdom occupied a position of vital strategic importance on the southern boundary of English Aquitaine. But England's diplomatic engagement with Charles II in 1370 failed to yield a definite agreement, perhaps reflecting his fears of attack from Castile and the pro-French elements in Aquitaine.[14] Having failed in the south, Edward III and his ministers looked to France's north-western flank, the independent duchy of Brittany. It was hoped that alliance with Brittany would help to compensate for the loss of Pembroke's expedition, and give English shipping access to more channel ports. Moreover, Duke Jean of Brittany himself resented the overspill of fighting across the boundaries of his duchy, and was particularly incensed by the conduct of the 'free companies', the notorious mercenary bands who formed a large part of the manpower on all sides of the conflict. But Duke Jean was also suspicious of Edward III, and had little intention of becoming his pawn in the broader struggle against France. Thus, the alliance that gradually developed between Edward III and Duke Jean was hedged with mutual suspicion and was never entirely wholehearted, in spite of the wording of the text of 19 July 1372 which committed both parties to a perpetual alliance against France.[15]

The concrete element to the arrangement was the promise of English military assistance, which was forthcoming in October 1372, when John, Lord Neville of Raby was contracted to lead a force of 600 men at a cost of £12,000. From the outset, Neville's expedition was plagued by difficulties; insufficient shipping delayed his departure until October, which was not a moment too soon for the people of Hampshire, who blamed a local a crime-wave on his restless and frustrated men. Whereas the despatch of Neville's army had been intended to shore-up de Montfort's position, the actual result was highly destabilising, as France reacted to the provocation by sending forces into Brittany from Poitou in the spring of 1373. By this time many of his leading subjects, including the bishop of Saint-Malo, were in open revolt, and Duke Jean was begging for further military aid from England. From June 1373 Neville's army was besieged at Brest by Bertrand de Guesclin, and it was clear that the Anglo-Breton military alliance was on the point of collapse. The failure of England's Breton strategy became manifest in May 1373 when Duke Jean fled to England as an exile.[16] The Breton debacle resulted in major recriminations over Neville's conduct, and these later resurfaced in The Good Parliament of 1376, when it was alleged that he had defrauded the crown by accepting wages for many more men than he had employed in his retinue, although the actual number that set foot in Brittany cannot be stated with certainty. Clearly, Neville was made a scapegoat for England's broader strategic failings, but it is worth noting that once again the conduct of the war was becoming a domestic political issue.[17]

In 1373 the council resolved once more to send a major expedition into France under the leadership of John of Gaunt. In July of that year Gaunt's expedition – the largest for many years – crossed to Calais. Gaunt's retinue included the duke of Brittany, the earls of Stafford, Suffolk and Warwick, Sir Hugh Calveley and Lord Percy, who between them captained 6,000 men, including 248 knights and more than 2,000 archers.[18] It is likely thatthe expedition had originally been intended to support the duke of Brittany, but his flight to England necessitated a change of objective. After disembarkation the army struck eastwards, crossing the Somme and the Aisne and ravaging the towns that lay in its path, probably with the intention of luring the French royal army to do battle. Wisely, Charles V and his captains avoided fighting a major battle, but Olivier de Clisson did succeed in mounting a successful ambush outside Sens. Deterred from advancing into Poitou, Gaunt progressed further southward, eventually wheeling towards the west and arriving in Bordeaux in December without encountering further serious opposition.[19] For all of its grandeur and the hundreds of miles of French territory that it covered, Gaunt's expedition of 1373 was characteristic of England's war effort throughout that entire decade – massively expensive and yielding few net gains in terms of territory recovered. And Gaunt's expedition was *truly* expensive, the outlay of £82,250 (as calculated by James Sherborne) being one of the single greatest items of English royal military expenditure of the century.[20] Although Gaunt had demonstrated England's ability to send an army across the length and breadth of France, he had neither brought the king of France to battle, nor had he recovered any of the county of Poitou. That Gaunt was no more of a failure than his contemporaries must be recognised, but, due to the increasing frailty of both his father and his elder brother, he was rapidly assuming the effective leadership of England's war effort, and the attendant burden of a kingdom's expectations.

April 1375 witnessed the last major English expedition into France of the reign of Edward III. The focus of English strategy once again returned to Brittany, and 4,000 men under Duke Jean de Montfort and the earl of Cambridge set out in April 1375. But this force spent little time in the field before it was announced that an Anglo-French truce had been agreed at Bruges, on 26 May 1375. Duke Jean felt that he had been sold-out by his English allies, and, in 1381, would conclude his own treaty with France.[21] In the two years that followed the Truce of Bruges English and French negotiators attempted to conclude a more durable arrangement, and the main issue on the table was a forty-year cessation of hostilities. By this time the focus of the most powerful man in England, John of Gaunt, had turned southwards to Castile. Since his marriage to Constance, the daughter of Pedro the Cruel, in 1371, Gaunt had harboured a strong interest in the succession to this kingdom, and had taken to styling himself as 'king of Castile' in his correspondence. Thus, as the life of Edward III ebbed away, England's great enterprise against France subsided into strategic lethargy, military failure, a loss of political will and the diversion of resources into the pursuit of personal aggrandisement.[22]

On 21 June 1377, Edward III died, and three days later, the two-year Anglo-French truce expired. Charles V's readiness for war and eagerness to maintain the strategic initiative became clear at the end of June when a Franco-Castilian fleet devastated the channel ports of Rye, Rottingdean, Weymouth, Dartmouth and Plymouth, and then returned to attack Southampton and Poole. Already suffering war weariness, the commons of England were gripped with renewed invasion hysteria, and a growing resentment against the royal council's manifest inability to protect the southern coastal towns. The raids on the south coast were also co-ordinated with a land offensive against Aquitaine under Louis, Duke of Anjou. By the middle of October the English-held parts of the duchy did not extend beyond the Bordelais – the town of Bordeaux, its hinterland and a coastal strip.[23] The accession of the ten-year-old Richard II, in July 1377, did nothing to revive England's military or diplomatic energies. The direction of the war had for some time been under the control of the late King's younger sons, John of Gaunt, Edmund of Langley and Thomas of Woodstock, as the Black Prince had been an invalid from before his return to England in 1371, until his death five years later.

The first major military expedition of the new reign was directed towards the destruction of the Franco-Castilian fleet moored at Sluys, and embarked under the leadership of Thomas of Woodstock in November 1377. Although there was no decisive engagement, by the end of 1377 England had gone some way to reasserting its military presence in the Channel.[24] Seeking to maintain this newly regained momentum, the royal council determined that a major expedition should sail in the new year of 1378. However, the organisation of this expedition proved to be very problematic, and its nominal commander, John of Gaunt, was still in England when his deputies, the Earls of Salisbury and Arundel, sailed for Harfleur. When Gaunt finally set sail in July, the advantage of surprise had been squandered, and the French fleet had already retreated up the Seine. In August Gaunt shifted his objective to St Malo, the capture of which would have brought some consolation for the failure of his mission's primary objective. Even this limited objective proved to be unobtainable, as the defenders were able to destroy the mine that the English engineers had been constructing under St Malo's walls. In September 1378 Gaunt returned to England, with his military reputation seriously tarnished.[25]

England's next foray had the more limited objective of offering military support to Charles of Navarre, much of whose kingdom had been occupied by the army of Henry of Trastamara, King of Castile. An army under Sir Thomas Trivet was despatched to Navarre in October 1378, but did not have to give battle, as the Castilians had withdrawn in advance of its arrival. The services of Trivet's army had come at a price, and Charles of Navarre's payment took the form of the cession of the port of Cherbourg, which came into English hands on 27 June 1379. The acquisition of this vital port had been well worth the service of 1,000 men for four months.[26]

But the successes in Navarre did little to restore the broader balance of military and diplomatic advantage in England's favour. Brittany, which had been under French occupation since 1373, held the key to restoring the balance of strategic power in the English Channel. With the exceptions of Brest and Cherbourg, Charles V had held Brittany with little difficulty, but his decision to annex it to the French crown, in December 1378, aroused a fierce response from the duchy's nobility, who urged the recall of Jean de Montfort. In spite of Duke Jean's lukewarm attitude to his English alliance, the royal council was enthusiastic to exploit Brittany as a springboard for an attack on Nantes.

The gravest impediment to the execution of this plan was financial, and it was not until August 1379 that the crown was able to secure funding for an expedition of 4,000 men, divided equally between men-at-arms and archers.[27] Planning for the expedition had been predicated on the assumption that the sum voted by Parliament would be available. But, in the localities, the royal commissioners were noticing an alarming shortfall between the local assessments and the actual sums collected, with the result that the expeditionary force had to be scaled down by more than two-thirds. Contrary winds delayed the embarkation of the expedition, and it was not until 6 December 1379 that Sir John Arundel, the Marshal of England, led his fleet into the Channel. One day later a storm of such ferocity blew up that the fleet was dispersed – Arundel himself drowning when his flagship ran aground off Ireland. No landing was made in Brittany, and the remnants of the English fleet returned home, with nothing to show for the expenditure of £15,000.[28]

The failure of Arundel's expedition further exacerbated the political tensions and insecurities in England. The continual council had shown itself to be an ineffectual manager of the war with France, and vast sums of money had been spent to little effect. At the beginning of 1380, the Chancellor, Richard, Lord Scrope, and the other members of the continual council resigned *en masse*, and were replaced by a new body headed by Simon Sudbury,

Archbishop of Canterbury (the governmental and political repercussions of the debacles of 1379–80 will be considered later in this
chapter). In spite of this dramatic change of personnel, Chancellor
Sudbury and his colleagues had inherited their predecessors' strategic priority of shoring up Duke Jean of Brittany against the French
military ascendancy. In January 1380, Parliament voted a subsidy for
a major expedition under the leadership of Thomas of Woodstock,
Earl of Buckingham, the youngest of the royal uncles. By the
middle of July, Earl Thomas had accumulated an army of more than
5,000 men, including contingents led by the veteran knights, Hugh
Calveley and Robert Knolles. This army had suffered none of the
material shortfalls of John Arundel's abortive expedition, and, when
it set out from Calais, it represented the greatest threat to the
French crown since John of Gaunt's *chevauchée* of 1373.

Although driving deep into France, first east towards the
Somme, and then south to Troyes, the expedition was unable to
bring the French to battle, as the Duke of Burgundy's army was
under strict orders to confine itself to shadowing Buckingham.
Moreover, on 16 September 1380, Charles V of France died, and
during the transition to the reign of his minor heir, the French
royal dukes continued their defensive footing. The arrival of
Buckingham's army in Rennes appeared to be met with indiffer-
ence by Duke Jean. No joint strategy was conceived by the two
men, and Buckingham turned his forces against the town of
Nantes. Unbeknown to Buckingham, who was making strenuous
efforts to convince the royal council to seek further parliamentary
funding, Duke Jean was already wavering in his loyalty, and, by the
beginning of 1381, had already reached a private accommodation
with the French. After a few desultory months in Brittany, the
English army set sail for home at the end of April 1381.[29]

Not a season had passed since the death of Edward III without a
major English expedition to France. During this period the
commitment of the royal council, the nobility, and the professional
soldiery to the French war cannot be doubted. Exhaustive efforts

were made to keep English armies in the field, and fleets at sea. Why so much planning and expenditure yielded so little military and diplomatic gain can be attributed to a number of factors. Much of English strategy had focused on Brittany, the duplicity of whose duke had hampered the application of a co-ordinated strategy. War by committee was also proving to be a frustrating exercise, and the absence of personal kingship, of the calibre that Charles V had been wielding in France, was sorely felt in England. Finally, England was cursed with the terrible luck of bad weather, which gravely hampered its naval operations in 1377 and 1379.

What impact did the failure of English arms have for the commons at this time? We should not underestimate the fears of those who were vulnerable to French attack, whether merchants-at-sea, or the inhabitants of coastal towns. During the Parliament held in the aftermath of the Great Rising in 1381, Sir Richard Waldegrave, Speaker of the Commons, noted the impunity with which France had attacked England's coastline, and adduced this as one of the main causes of popular rebellion.[30] In a more general sense, the military and diplomatic reversals of the period since Edward III's death had created a widespread crisis of confidence in the ability of the young King's councillors to protect the kingdom, to advance its strategic aims, and to uphold the honour and reputation of England, that had been so dearly bought by the previous generation. The sudden changes to the personnel of government at the beginning of 1380 were taken as a desperate measure to restore parliamentary confidence in the King's advisers.

Whatever the fear and national shame felt by the commons of England, their most strongly felt grievances were financial. The substantial reduction in the size of Sir Thomas Trivet's expedition of 1378 was a compelling indication of how the tail of crown finance was wagging the dog of military strategy. For the previous century, the English crown had depended upon the levy on moveable goods to fund its armies. The recourse to the infamous Poll Taxes of 1377, 1379 and 1380 was an admission both of the exhaustion of the traditional sources of revenue, and a mismatch between the ambitions of the royal council's strategy and the inadequacies of its fiscal base. Although the significance of the three Poll Taxes will be considered later in this chapter, it is perhaps worth reflecting whether there would have been such a violent antipathy to this fiscal innovation had one of the expeditions of this period succeeded in delivering an overwhelming victory comparable to those that had been achieved in the 1340s and 1350s.

KING, COURT AND PARLIAMENT

It is something of a truism to say that England was a monarchy, and kings were expected to rule. But the absence of an effective king from the mid-1370s until the early 1380s lay at the heart of England's domestic political crises. Ideally, an ageing king would have an adult and capable son, who, after a suitable apprenticeship-in-arms and administration, would be chafing to succeed his father. The 'model' transition was that of 1272, when Edward I succeeded his ageing father, Henry III. The final years of Edward I's reign had been characterised by tension between the King and his heir, the future Edward II, over the exile of his hated companion, Piers Gaveston. Although succeeding to a discredited and weakened kingship, Edward III set the tone for his reign by his violent overthrow of the unpopular regime of his mother Isabella, and her lover, Roger Mortimer. In spite of the contrasting circumstances of the successions of the three Edwards, they were all of an age to take on the mantle of kingship.

The succession in 1377 differed from the previous three due to a dynastic discontinuity within the English royal family. In the 1360s, England had been set to have two further Edwards on its throne, making a consecutive run of five. Edward, the 'Black Prince', had been born in 1330, and, by the time that he had reached his mid-thirties was serving his regal apprenticeship in Aquitaine. In 1365,

Edward and Joan of Kent had their first son, who would have succeeded as Edward V. Like Henry VIII and Charles I, Richard II was not born to be king, and he spent the first four years of his life as a younger son. By the time that Richard II had become heir presumptive to the English crown, on the death of his brother Edward in 1371, their father was in a very fragile state of health. That same year, aged only forty, the Black Prince returned to England, and, for the last five years of his life, played a negligible role in politics and government.

Had Edward III remained in sound health in his later years, then the eventual transition to his grandson would have posed few problems. But, by the early 1370s, Edward III was slipping into a degenerative state that would become a severe dementia. The absence of personal kingship was exacerbated by the fact that Edward III had outlived almost all of the military companions of his own generation. How the vacuum of personal kingship came to be filled would destroy the domestic political consensus that had prevailed for many years, and bequeath to the subsequent reign a bitter legacy of political faction and popular suspicion of the King's household, the royal bureaucracy and the city of London – and the personalities operating at its nexus.

The chief personalities in the scandal that rocked the final months of Edward III's reign stood at the points of a corrupt triangle – Alice Perrers, the royal mistress, William Latimer, the King's chamberlain, and Sir Richard Lyons, a city financier. After a career-in-arms, William Latimer became steward of the royal household in 1368, and, two years later, its chamberlain. One of the main functions of this office was to handle the loans, often running into tens of thousands of pounds, that bridged the deficit between the yield of taxation and actual military expenditure. However, Latimer was more than merely the receiver of the loans, he also brokered credit for the crown through a leading city financier, Richard Lyons. By the middle of the 1370s, Latimer and Lyons had become the 'usual channels' through which the wealth of the mercantile elite was tapped for war credit. Whereas funds that passed through the Exchequer were subject to rigorous auditing, the King's chamber was a self regulating organ that had evolved to handle the high volumes of cash flow necessary to pay the crown's military contractors.[31] The charmed circle was completed by the figure of Alice Perrers, who had emerged from obscurity as royal mistress in the early 1370s, and had already borne an illegitimate son to the King. Like the great royal mistresses of the Renaissance or the Bourbon ascendancy, Alice derived her authority from her ability to control access to, and influence, the person of the King. The sensitivity of the position of Latimer, Lyons and Perrers lay in the widespread perception among the members of the House of Commons that, through a combination of incompetence and personal corruption, they had mismanaged and dissipated the subsidies that had been voted to sustain the military expeditions of 1372–6.

Hostility against the court exploded in May 1376, when Parliament met to answer royal demands for new subsidies. The objections of the Commons were articulated by Sir Peter de la Mare, who is credited with being the first Speaker. De la Mare broadened his criticisms into a damning indictment of the leading courtiers. The principal charge against Lyons and Latimer was that they had raised 20,000 marks of capital in order to lend it to the crown at the extortionate premium of 50%. It was also alleged that they had conspired to block a much more competitive offer from William Walworth (later mayor during the 1381 revolt) and Adam Francis, who were ready to advance 15,000 marks without any premium. At the other end of the credit equation, Latimer and Lyons were alleged to have bought up debts owing to the crown at a fraction of their full value, and then traded them for their own profit. Alice Perrers was directly accused of bleeding the household of more than £2,000 annually for her personal profit, and her removal from the King's presence was urged.[32]

By the end of May, Latimer had been placed in the custody of the Marshal of England, and Lyons imprisoned. Although less closely implicated in the worst excesses of the corruption, John, Lord Neville of Raby was dismissed from the stewardship of the Household, and Adam Bury, a former mayor of Calais and collector of customs, was similarly disgraced. The public impeachment of the most senior of the King's household officers must have gravely shaken the faith of taxpayers in the town and countryside alike. The morale of the court was lowered further on 8 June 1376, when the Black Prince died. By the time that Parliament had been prorogued, a little over a month later, only a three-year grant of the customs had been conceded, and the desired vote of a full subsidy had been withheld. In the short-term, the enemies of the court had won.[33]

By the autumn of 1376 it had become clear that while the King lived his intimate advisors and councillors continued to enjoy his protection. On 8 October Latimer was pardoned, and, soon after, Alice Perrers was acquitted of any sums owing to the Household. The moving force behind this retaliation was by now also the most influential figure at court, John of Gaunt, Duke of Lancaster. In the following Parliament of January 1377, Gaunt regained much of the initiative for the court, and stamped its authority over military and diplomatic strategy. Perhaps the most evocative symbol of the court's triumph was Peter de la Mare's incarceration in Nottingham Castle, far away from the Chapter House in Westminster where he had made his reputation the previous year. Thomas Walsingham even claimed that Gaunt had planned to execute de la Mare in the woods outside Nottingham Castle, and would have done so but for the intervention of Lord Percy.[34] By the end of Hilary Parliament, in April 1377, all of the impeached men of the previous year, including Lyons and Bury, had received a royal pardon.

In the eyes of many Englishmen, John of Gaunt had become an overbearing and uncontrollable presence within the polity. In his *Vision of Piers Plowman*, Langland made an allegory of the conflict between the Commons and the court:

> *A rabble of rats ran suddenly hither*
> *With a swarm of small mice sporting among them.*
> *They came to a council for the common profit.*
> *A cat of the court would come at his pleasure*
> *Sport and spring and seize whom he fancied.*
> *Play with them perilously and push them before him.*
> *We dread the danger and dare not come forward,*
> *And if we grudge him his game he will grieve us further,*
> *Scratch us or claw us or take us in his clutches,*
> *And make life loathsome before he leave us.*
> *If we had the wit to withstand his pleasure*
> *We might be lords aloft and live at our leisure.*[35]

As Edward III lay dying, both 'the cat of the court' and 'the mice' doubtless wondered how the succession of a boy-king would influence their struggle for power.

THE GOVERNANCE OF ENGLAND IN RICHARD II'S MINORITY

The accession to the throne of England of a ten-year-old boy in July 1377 posed obvious problems for the governance of the kingdom. The last comparable minority succession had been in 1216, when the kingdom of England had passed to the infant Henry III. As much of southern England had been under French occupation, the appointment of a regent, William the Marshal, had been a military necessity. Although English fortunes were in a deep trough in July 1377, there was no similar imperative to institute a regency. Moreover, the only candidate with an unequalled seniority of blood was the one whose appointment would have re-opened the deepest of the wounds of 1376.

John of Gaunt's worst enemies, including Charles V of France, were not far short of alleging that he was planning to displace his nephew as Edward III's heir and successor. Thomas Walsingham, who was seldom favourably disposed to the Duke, alleged that in 1376 he had attempted to seek a statutory bar on any claim to the throne transmitted through a female. This could only have been directed at his rival Edmund Mortimer, Earl of March, who was married to the daughter of Gaunt's deceased elder brother, Lionel, Duke of Clarence. Mortimer had been one of the most determined sponsors of the Good Parliament's campaign against the court, and the Speaker, Sir Peter de la Mare, was his steward. Although Gaunt was clearly jockeying for power throughout 1376-7, there was nothing in his actions to support a treasonable construction of his ambitions. In spite of his loyalty to the succession of his brother's son, Gaunt's taste for confrontational politics gave his enemies plenty of ammunition during the sensitive period of transition in the closing months of Edward III's life.[36]

The dispute that brought Gaunt into conflict with the people of London (which would later have disastrous consequences for his property in the city in 1381) centred on the connected issues of taxation of the Church and the legal privileges of the city. One of the novelties of the First Poll Tax of 1377 (which will be considered in greater detail below) was that it included the clergy. Their intense resistance to inclusion in the tax sparked a war of words with the Duke. Gaunt's leading ecclesiastical opponent was William Wykeham, Bishop of Winchester, and the two had already clashed in the Parliament of the previous year. The respect with which Wykeham was regarded made him a formidable opponent to the Duke. In order to strengthen his cause, Gaunt drafted in the services of a former diplomat and Oxford theologian, John Wycliffe, who had already attracted considerable attention for his views on ecclesiastical wealth, lay magistracy over the church, and papal authority. As Wycliffe found himself in increasingly choppy political waters, Gaunt assumed the role of his protector.

In the early months of 1377, Wycliffe's views appeared to be gaining currency among elements within the Commons and the

Lords. When Wycliffe advocated greater exploitation of the Church's wealth to meet the recurrent emergencies of the French war he was preaching to the converted. The inevitable reaction from the Church was both severe and dramatic. On 19 February 1377 Wycliffe was brought to St Paul's to account for his views before William Courtenay, Bishop of London.[37]

In this collision between the interests of Church and state, a deftness of political touch was called for on all sides. However, Gaunt appeared to regard the questioning of his *protégé* as an effort to try him by proxy, and his reaction was characteristically forceful. Whether or not Gaunt threatened to drag the Bishop from his office by the roots of his hair, as Walsingham would have us believe, the hearing rapidly degenerated into a riot. By this stage, Gaunt had clearly made his point, but, in the face of further protests from the Londoners, he went on to threaten a suspension of the city's liberties, and the appointment of a royal governor.

The popular reaction to Gaunt's heavy-handed intervention in London affairs was an ominous sign of the degree of anger and alienation felt within the capital. On the following day, the mayor and aldermen argued bitterly with the Duke's leading servants about the liberties of the city, and it would seem that at least one Londoner was arrested for slandering Gaunt and his close ally, Henry, Lord Percy. Indeed, there was a rumour circulating in the city that the Duke was the changeling son of a Ghentish butcher. That evening, Gaunt and Percy were attacked while dining in the home of the Duke's servant, Sir John d'Ypres, and they barely escaped with their lives by rowing across the river to Kennington, where the future king and his mother were residing. The degree of popular hatred for Gaunt can be gathered from the fact that his servants were reportedly afraid to wear his livery in public. The disturbances in London were eventually calmed by the Bishop, and, somewhat belatedly, the ailing King summoned the leading Londoners to attend him at Sheen.[38]

Had Gaunt shown the magnanimity expected of a great prince, then perhaps his relationship with the Londoners could have been repaired. However, his reaction to the deputation of Londoners betrayed fear and insecurity rather than a command of the situation. As the price for his pardon, he demanded the erection in Cheapside of a marble pillar surmounted by his arms – probably as a public penance for the defacement to which they had been subjected throughout the city. He also demanded that the mayor and alder-men make a penitential procession to St Paul's, and that those of their number who had colluded in the disturbances be dismissed. Gaunt did receive an apology, and selected officers were dismissed, but the corporation declined to abase itself publicly. It was doubtless clear to both the Duke and the Londoners alike that the issues between them were far from resolved, and that the legacy of their confrontation was one of growing bitterness and mutual suspicion.[39]

The death of Edward III, on 21 June 1377, brought to the fore-front of politics the question of the Duke's position in government, and his relationship with his nephew, now King Richard II. It would seem that the Duke realised that his father's death entailed an inevitable diminution of his power, especially in the capital. A reconciliation was orchestrated between the Duke and the Londoners, in which the young Richard II played the princely role of mediator and honest-broker. A few days after the coronation, Gaunt officially withdrew from court, with the apparent intention of turning his mind to the management of his landed estates.[40]

Between July 1377 and January 1380, England was ruled by continual councils which had full executive authority. In October 1377, the Commons petitioned that the councils be appointed in Parliament. This was more than merely a desire for public trans-parency, and is suggestive of a fear among the Commons that the council could fall under the control of the court. The first council consisted of nine bishops, earls, barons and bannerets (senior knights entitled to bear a square banner in war), and it was stipulated that they should serve for only one year, without the prospect of renewal. The intention was to create a broadly based council that was accountable to Parliament, and staffed by men of experience.[41]

The leading lay figures on the council were the Earls of March (who had offered strong support to the Commons against the court in 1376) and Arundel, one of the greatest landowners in the kingdom. The leading churchman was Bishop Courtenay of London, who had clashed publicly with Gaunt earlier that same year.

The most notable absentees from the council of July 1377 were the King's uncles, (two of whom, Buckingham and Cambridge, were serving in arms) and, especially, John of Gaunt. As has been noted, the Duke retired officially from the court shortly after his nephew's coronation. However, to have completely marginalised the interests of the King's heir apparent, and the most powerful man in the kingdom, would have been politically counter-productive. When the council of July 1377 was constituted it included two men associated with Gaunt, his former chancellor, Ralph Erghum, now bishop of Salisbury, and Sir William Windsor. This latter appointment was particularly obnoxious to the Commons, who regarded Windsor as a key figure in the court scandal of the previous year, and he was duly excluded from the council when it was re-constituted in December 1377.[42]

Although lacking an official role in the continual councils, Gaunt tended to act as a 'political lightning conductor'. More than ten years before, during the Black Prince's Castilian campaign, two esquires in the service of Sir John Chandos, Robert Hawley and John Shakel, had taken captive the Count of Denia. In exchange for his freedom, the Count had surrendered his son to be held as hostage in England as a surety for the payment of his ransom. Following Richard II's succession, the council had granted the custody of the son to John of Gaunt, who claimed to be king of Castile, by right of his wife, Constance, the daughter of Pedro the Cruel. Unwilling to surrender their hostage the two squires were committed to the Tower of London, but escaped to Westminster, where they claimed sanctuary in the Abbey. A botched effort to recapture the squires, undertaken by Sir Alan Buxhill, constable of the Tower and Sir Ralph Ferrers, resulted in the murder of Hawley and a sacristan of the Abbey. In the uproar that followed, Bishop Courtenay of London excommuni-cated Buxhill and Ferrers. Thomas Walsingham attributed Gaunt's sudden denunciation of Bishop Courtenay to his supposed collusion in, and instigation of, the action to arrest the two esquires. Although Walsingham was ready to paint Gaunt in the worst light, and to support the most unflattering construction of his actions, there can be little doubt that the Duke was further tainted by perceptions of his involvement in the affair.[43]

The third and final continual council, appointed in November 1378, differed considerably in its composition, the most notable new appointee being Bishop Wykeham of Winchester, who had opposed Gaunt in 1377. The Earl of Arundel returned to office, and the ageing Earl of Suffolk was also included. However, the most significant new appointment was Sir Aubrey de Vere, a leading royal household knight. Although there is no single discernible trend in the council's composition – as some appointments cancelled each other out in political terms – the interests of John of Gaunt appear to have been gradually edged to the periphery. Given the disastrous state of the war, and of the rising unpopularity of the crown's fiscal policies, the Duke may have been thankful for his distance from the royal council.

THE POLL TAXES

Would there have been a popular revolt in England without the three Poll Taxes of 1377, 1379 and 1380? It is clear that the first three years of Richard II's reign were a dismal catalogue of military humiliations abroad and political factionalism at home. The fears of Franco-Castilian raids, or a full-scale invasion, created an atmos-phere of fear and suspicion throughout the southern counties of England. Moreover, the political traumas surrounding the deaths of Edward III and the Black Prince, and the conflicts between the court and the Commons, compounded popular fears.

The Poll Taxes, and the collection of the Third Poll Tax in particular, proved to be the immediate cause of the Great Rising. Although a completely novel fiscal experiment, the Poll Taxes should be seen in the context of a growing burden of royal fiscal demands, imposed within a highly regressive framework, throughout the fourteenth century.

Before 1377 the English crown had relied on the 'lay subsidy', which taxed the value of a proportion of each household's moveable property, usually a 'fifteenth'. The immunity of land and capital from taxation ensured that the wealthiest were cushioned most from the crown's rising fiscal demands. Whatever its inequalities, the lay subsidy had been a broadly effective means of raising money to fund Edward III's wars. Why, therefore, did the crown not simply seek further subsidies in their traditional form? The principal reason for the abandonment of the lay subsidy in 1377–80 lay in the population decline following the Black Death. Assessments for the lay subsidy had not been changed since 1334, with the result that in the decades of post-Black Death depopulation, many communities found it impossible to satisfy the sums demanded. By the late 1370s the composition of many communities bore little resemblance to their assessments, due to population movements and dramatic shifts in wealth. Therefore in 1377 the crown's most pressing concern was to bring as much of the population within its fiscal reach.[44]

On 2 February 1377 Parliament assembled at Westminster, summoned in the name of the dying Edward III, but most probably at the instigation of the Duke of Lancaster. First the Chancellor elaborated the necessity of raising further taxes for the defence of the realm, as costs were mounting (so he claimed) on a daily basis. The Chancellor then demanded 4d from every male and female, over the age of fourteen, regardless of their degree, excepting only beggars.[45] Regrettably, there are no surviving minutes for the royal council to allow a more detailed tracing of the formulation of the first flat-rate capitation tax in British history. The tax yielded £22,000, and there appeared to be no resistance to its collection.[46]

Whether the tax was intended to be a one-off, or the basis of a new method of raising revenue to supersede the traditional lay subsidy, was never made clear. Perhaps the apparent success of the tax encouraged the Chancellor, Lord Scrope, and his fellow councillors to repeat the exercise, in the desperate months following John of Gaunt's failure to capture St Malo. On 27 April 1379 Parliament opened, and, as before, the crown outlined the necessity of raising another subsidy. In its novelty, the Second Poll Tax is as striking and as unusual as the first. The flat-rate capitation was replaced with an elaborate sliding scale.

For the purposes of 'banding' the population was divided into seven categories: (1) landowners from duke down to esquire; (2) knights of the international crusading orders; (3) men of law; (4) townsmen, municipal officers and merchants; (5) notaries, legal apprentices, pardoners, common married men and women; (6) foreign merchants; and (7) all religious from archbishops down to monks and nuns. All told, there were about fifty separate categories, ranging from dukes and archbishops (£6 13s 4d) down to simple men and women, and poor monks and nuns (4d). The parallel nature of the banding system of 1379 tells us much about the changing balance of wealth and status in late medieval England. Mayors of larger towns were assessed at the same rate (40s) as barons, a concept unthinkable fifty years earlier. Although lauded by historians for its progressiveness, this tax proved to be disappointing for the royal council, as it yielded only £18,600, more than £3,000 less than in 1377.[47] Corruption in the administration of the tax, possibly involving the bribing of collectors to depress individual assessments, had brought down the yield. But the real inadequacy of the 1379 tax yield becomes clear when it is compared to the actual costs of keeping an army in the field. During the first half of that year, the wage bill for Gaunt's army had been £50,000.[48]

The genesis of the infamous and controversial Third Poll Tax of 1380 can be located in a combination of military desperation, and a change of personnel at the top of government, with the appointment of a new Chancellor, Archbishop Sudbury. The Parliament that voted the Third Poll Tax opened at Northampton on 5 November 1380. Weeks of atrocious autumn weather had brought widespread flooding, and even the King himself had experienced difficulty in completing the simple journey from London to Northampton. The travel experiences of churchmen, lords and knights from further afield can only be guessed at. It was not just the weather that thinned out the ranks of those attending Parliament. Tension on the Scottish borders had caused the despatch there of the Duke of Lancaster, with a special rank of King's Lieutenant on the Marches, and a retinue including many knights and noblemen.

On 8 November 1380 the King, now aged thirteen, entered the priory of St Andrews. Following what was by now a well-established pattern, the new Chancellor, Archbishop Sudbury, rehearsed the necessity for the calling of the Parliament. As in 1379, the Chancellor painted a bleak picture of an English army (that of the King's uncle Buckingham) stranded without sufficient funds to meet its wages, and the potential for military humiliation at the hands of the kingdom's enemies. England's fiscal crisis was further exacerbated by a revolt in the Flemish manufacturing towns – the main destination for England's wool exports. In 1379, the townsmen of the great manufacturing centres of Bruges, Ghent and Ypres began a revolt against the lordship of Louis de Mâle, Count of Flanders. The sudden crash in the demand for the exports of English wool had a knock-on effect for the wool subsidy, the yields of which collapsed.[49]

Time and again, the Chancellor repeated the national humiliation that would result from the crown defaulting on its debts, with the possible result of jeopardising the crown jewels, which had already been surrendered as security. It was clear that Chancellor Sudbury was laying the ground for a very substantial demand for taxation – but no-one was actually prepared for the sum of £160,000 when it came. Astonished by the scale of the subsidy, the Commons referred the demand back to the Lords, with the demand that the Upper House provide alternative suggestions for the raising of the sum.

After further debate, the Lords made three proposals for the collection of the tax. The two options that were not adopted would, unsurprisingly, have been the most burdensome for the Commons, and the gentle and mercantile classes that they represented. One was the imposition of a 'poundage' – a tax that would have applied to all sales within the kingdom. Another option was the granting of multiple subsidies on moveable goods, until £160,000 were collected.

In the event, the Commons voted for a return to a flat-rate capitation, with 12d to be levied on every man and woman over the age of fifteen. Not only was this three times the imposition of 1377, but it also fell most harshly upon those least able to pay. Moreover, as Fryde points out, in 1379 married men and women were able to divide their tax liability of 4d (a primitive form of married persons' tax relief), thereby halving the individual burden, whereas in 1380 no such allowance was made.[50]

Responsibility for the inception of such a provocative and manifestly unjust tax falls on a number of shoulders. The 1380 tax could have been avoided had the crown tailored its military ambitions to its straitened fiscal circumstances. By continuing with its tactics of costly but fruitless expeditions, the royal council was throwing good money after bad. Secondly, the royal council and the lords could have offered firmer guidance about the potential consequences arising from a trebled flat-rate capitation. Finally, the willingness of the Commons to off-load the bulk of the fiscal burden on to the unrepresented masses was a decision of monumental political short-sightedness.

However, there was one dissenting voice at the very centre of the political nexus. Shortly after the dissolution of the 1380 Parliament, Thomas Brantingham, Bishop of Exeter, resigned the treasurership of England. In 1326 his predecessor in both offices, Walter Stapledon, had been lynched by a London mob, who held him responsible for the hated financial policies of Edward II. If Brantingham had not been alone in realising the tendency of history to repeat itself, then perhaps the 1381 revolt could still have been averted.

THE COLLECTION AND ENFORCEMENT OF
THE 1380 POLL TAX

Tax-raising in medieval England was carried out through the largely devolved structure of local government. Collectors were appointed for each county, and sub-collectors for individual villages and towns, supported by constables, mayors and bailiffs. Therefore the process of collection demanded the services of royal officials, municipal authorities and village constables, acting in their own localities.

The initial response of the English people to the imposition of the Third Poll Tax was not violence, but evasion. When British local authorities were collecting the Poll Tax of 1990, they noted dramatic reductions of the numbers on the electoral rolls. More than 130,000 people disappeared from the London electoral rolls alone in the year 1989–90.[51] Perhaps unwittingly, the tens of thousands of individuals who evaded registration in 1989–90 were imitating their forebears of the winter of 1380–81.

The extent and degree of evasion of the Third Poll Tax of 1380 was first considered by Charles Oman more than a century ago. By comparing the number of tax-payers registered for the First Poll Tax (1377) with those registered for the third, he found that 458,720 adult men and women had disappeared from the rolls, more than one-third of those liable to pay. The reduction in numbers was particularly striking in the heavily populated counties closest to London, where the surveys are likely to have been the most comprehensive. In Kent the numbers enrolled had dropped by twenty-two per cent, in Norfolk twenty-five per cent, in Bedfordshire twenty-seven per cent, in Berkshire thirty-one per cent, and in Essex a staggering thirty-six per cent. These counties were later those with the highest concentrations of disorder in 1381.

How did the concealment occur? Oman observed that the 1380 lists showed an unusual preponderance of males, which suggests that households may have concealed the existence of un-married females and widows, or under-declared the ages of girls aged fifteen and over.

Given the fact the sub-collectors would have been aware of the composition of the households in their own communities, then a substantial degree of collusion may have occurred in these evasions.[52]

Initially, the collectors had been commissioned to secure payment of two-thirds of the payments by January 1381, and the remaining third by the following June. However, by the end of December 1380 the shortfall apparent in the initial sums collected caused the royal council to order inquiries into the evasion of the tax, on 2 January 1381.[34]

By 20 February the Exchequer was becoming increasingly alarmed by the deficit between their estimates and the actual sums collected, with the result that the royal council ordered the collectors to renew their efforts. When the collectors reported their findings they attributed the shortfall to systematic evasion, with the result that, on 16 March, new commissions were appointed to track down the missing taxpayers.[35] The commissioners were to interrogate the municipal and village authorities, under oath, to ascertain which households had concealed members liable to taxation. Little imagination is required to imagine the tension and fear engendered in a system of detection reliant upon a combination of denunciation and self-incrimination.

Although the council was not oblivious to the prospect of physical resistance to the collection of the tax, it would seem that it anticipated little more than isolated and individual acts of opposition. Through a combination of perseverance and intimidation, the commissioners were gradually recovering the shortfall from those communities that had under-declared their liabilities. The two figures behind this determined drive were the Chancellor, Archbishop Sudbury, and the new Treasurer, Sir Robert Hales.

There can be little doubt that the causes of the 1381 revolt lie in a combination of factors, some of which can be traced back to the agrarian crises of the beginning of the fourteenth century. The main immediate cause of the outbreak of the revolt has long been regarded as the Third Poll Tax of 1380, and the extraordinary measures that were used to enforce its collection in the following spring. But the crown's fiscal demands were not the only causes of revolt. Ever since the resurgence of war in 1369, England had found itself in a downward spiral of diplomatic failure and military defeat.

Had the English crown and the royal council governed in a way that commanded the respect of the people, the reversals in the French war might have been more bearable. However, the final months of Edward III's reign had left a legacy of corruption, recrimination and profound mistrust within the political establishment. Even before his father's death John of Gaunt, Duke of Lancaster, had become the *bête noire* of the Commons due to his defence of corrupt courtiers, and heavy-handed intervention in the politics of London. His own public withdrawal from the royal council in July 1377 was, in part, a recognition of his unpopularity as well as a desire to distance himself from the repercussions of future failures which, he feared (and not without justification), would be laid at his door. This general malaise and discontent further aggravated the existing tensions in the English countryside. The suddenness with which revolt took hold in the late spring of 1381 should not diminish the role played by a powerful combination of long-term causes – fiscal, economic, military and political.

3

THE REBELS AND
THEIR AIMS

LEADERS AND LED

The revolt that broke out in the villages of Kent and Essex at the beginning of the second week of June 1381 had social, economic and political origins stretching back for many years, and, in some cases, decades. Before following the course of the Rising, it is necessary to consider what forms the movement took, and the relationship between the participants and the men who were named by contemporaries as their leaders.

There are few commoners in English history who have left a more lasting imprint on the popular consciousness than the leaders of the Great Rising of 1381. Wat Tyler and Jack Straw have been immortalised in street names and pub signs. But, the greater the focus on the identities of the leaders, and the dynamics of their influence and control, the more blurred is the resulting picture. To what extent were the men named as the leaders of the revolt in London able to direct the actions of their own followers, and those participants in the concurrent risings in the counties? Did the leaders of the rebels in East Anglia and the southern counties look to the London rebels, or were they largely autonomous in their actions?

The question of the rebels' motivations is no less complex. Although the demands made by Wat Tyler of Richard II are well known, the extent to which he was speaking for all who rose is far from clear. Disentangling the local grievances of the rebels outside London from any broader shared agenda is difficult, and, also, perhaps a misunderstanding of the dynamics of protest. It is dangerous to rationalise the apparent contradictions and distinctions between the various stated objectives of the rebels in the search for a coherent, but ultimately misleading, 'common manifesto'. Rather, the Great Rising is distinctive precisely because of the plurality of its patterns of violence, and the broad social range of its participants. In spite of the enduring fame of the rebel leaders there is a serious dearth of information about their lives before 1381, when they leapt to prominence in the accounts of the contemporary chroniclers. The principal accounts often list variations of the spellings of their surnames, and are keen to report their individual words and deeds.

Most of the contemporary sources credit Wat Tyler with the single most important individual role in the revolt, and all the sources concur that he came from Kent, while the compiler of the *Anonimalle Chronicle* located him to Maidstone. Thomas Walsingham places him at the head of a list of the Rising's leaders, while Jean Froissart was emphatic in identifying him as the paramount leader of the Commons of the south-eastern counties, but it is possible that this fame was amplified by his famous encounter with Richard II.[1] The *Anonimalle Chronicle* suggests that the impetus behind his leadership was some form of primitive popular election, rather than his own ambition. Walsingham regarded Tyler as the intellectual force behind the movement, and credited him with a radical manifesto of regicide, destruction of the royal council, the nobility and the city of London. When compared to the other reports of Tyler's demands, Walsingham's allegations of Tyler's designs lack credibility. Indeed, the *Anonimalle Chronicle* credited him with a populist royalism and stated that his followers used as their challenge, 'With whom haldes yow?' to which the correct response was 'Wyth King Richarde and wyth the trew communes'.[2]

At the centre of the revolt there is the puzzling question of the nature of Tyler's leadership. Was he merely *primus inter pares*, the most famous and charismatic of the leaders, slain at the height of the Rising in London? Or was he able to communicate a personal leadership, both within London and to the rebels farther afield? The written communications issued by the rebels, and the subsequent trials of Londoners who had colluded in the invasion of the capital, show that there would have been many literate men among their number.

Some clue to the dynamics of Tyler's position within the Rising can be gathered from Thomas Walsingham's lengthy digression into the events in his own town of St Albans. For almost a century the status of the town of St Albans had been fought over by the abbots, who asserted that the town was part of their manor and, the townsmen, who considered themselves to be burgesses, and autonomous of the Abbey. Although the townsmen themselves were capable of inflicting considerable damage upon the Abbey's possessions, their ultimate objective was official, external recognition of their autonomy.

The events of 1381 in St Albans were a near repetition of those in 1326–7, when the townsmen had a obtained a confirmation of their free status issued in the name of Edward III. This time they marched on London again, but in addition to seeking letters from the young King, they also went in search of Wat Tyler, 'to receive power from him, as they believed no one in the future would have as much power in him in the kingdom, as the laws of the land would have no force'.[3] Walsingham then adds that one of the leaders of the St Albans men, William Grindecobbe, had an interview with Tyler, in which he persuaded him to send an army of 20,000 men to kill the Abbot and monks, and destroy the Abbey, in the event of their continued intransigence. Tyler reportedly agreed to this, on the condition that the men of St Albans accepted his leadership, without question.

If there is any truth to this account, penned by the bitterest of the enemies of the St Albans townsmen, then it casts some light on the dynamics of the revolt, and on the relationship between the rebels in London, and those outside. If the St Albans men did regard Tyler, even in a vague way, as the future ruler of England, it would suggest their own local pre-occupations did not blind them to the potential of a total re-ordering of government and political society. Furthermore, the decision of the St Albans men to seek Tyler's leadership suggests a hunger for external direction. It might be suggested that while the leaders of the revolt were conspicuously destroying the established economic and social hierarchies, they were also seeking to build new relationships of authority and dependency between the capital and the counties.

After Tyler, the rebel leader whose identity seems most certain is the radical preacher John Ball. All of the sources concur that John Ball had established a reputation in Kent for his preaching some years before the Great Rising. Ball has fascinated theologians, philosophers and historians for centuries due to the radical egalitarianism of the speeches and letters that have been attributed to him. Perhaps the most famous of these is the rhyme, 'When Adam delved and Eve span, Who then was a gentleman?' Both high Royalists, including Charles I himself, and Puritan polemicists, identified echoes of the Great Rising in the political discourse of the mid-seventeenth century.[4] In the 1790s John Ball was adopted as a totemic figure by English radicals, and he was lauded by writers as diverse as Friedrich Engels, in his works on class conflict in the early modern period, and William Morris in *The Dream of John Ball*.

There are however, considerable disparities in the contemporary accounts of Ball's role in the Rising. Froissart regarded him as the leading instigator of the entire Rising, and drew a causal link between his radical preaching and the outbreak of popular violence. For Froissart, Ball's preaching inflamed the Londoners, causing disturbances in the city that only later spread to the adjacent counties. However, none of the other sources affords Ball such a prominent role. In Henry Knighton's *Chronicle* John Ball is rescued from the Archbishop of Canterbury's prison at Maidstone by a crowd of Kentishmen who had assembled at Blackheath. The connection between Ball and the Kentish rebels cannot be doubted, but it would seem that he had actually been released from custody before the gathering at Blackheath, rather than being sprung by an attack on the archiepiscopal gaol at Maidstone. Knighton's claim that the rebels 'intended to make him their Archbishop' is very significant, as G.H. Martin has noted that the *Anonimalle Chronicle* recorded one of Tyler's main demands as being that there should be 'but one bishop and one prelate in England'.[5] How easily Ball's radical egalitarian preaching could be reconciled with his supposed ambition to be a kind of metropolitan over the entire English Church was never explained.

John Ball stands out in the history of popular protest as the first rebel leader to commit his ideology to paper. The 1381 Rising generated a small but remarkable cycle of political verses written in rhyming English couplets. Although Ball's authorship can never be proven, both the chroniclers Henry Knighton and Thomas Walsingham, who may even have witnessed Ball's execution at St Albans, copied the letters into their narratives. Whether the letters were verses composed for the rebels' amusement, or political allegories, or coded instructions to incite resistance, cannot be known. But they do give a unique flavour of the mix of political anger and quasi-millenarian prophecy that suffused the rebels' ideology. This excerpt from the verses appears in Walsingham, and a similar version can also be found in Knighton:

> *John the Miller hath ground small, small, small:*
> *The King's son of heaven shall pay for all,*
> *Beware or be ye woe,*
> *Know your friend from your foe,*
> *Have enough and say 'Ho!'*
> *And do well and better, and flee sin,*
> *And seek peace and hold you therein*
> *And so biddeth John Trewman and all his fellows.*[6]

The extended version of the verses, quoted in Knighton's *Chronicle*, is a cycle in which Jack Miller, Jack Trewman and Jack Carter each give a speech of exhortation. Jack Carter's speech seems to direct the rebels to further acts of violence:

> Jack Carter prays you all that you make a good end of what you have begun, and do well, and ever better, for in the evening a man reckons the day. For if the end be well, then all is well. Let Piers Ploughman my brother stay at home and get us corn, and I will go with you, and help as I can to prepare your meat and drink, so that you lack not. See that Hob the Robber be well punished for losing your grace, for you have great need to take God with you in all that you do. For now is the time to take care.[7]

Much critical ink has been expended on the questions of whether 'Piers Plowman' had any connection with William Langland's literary creation, and whether 'Hob the Robber' was Sir Robert Hales, or some other figure demonised by the rebels. However, their significance lies more in the glimpse that they give us into a lost mental landscape, populated with serfs and ploughmen, and evoking a simplistic folkloric Christianity.[8] Unique among known leaders of the revolt, Ball is identified in the letters, and addresses the people of England directly:

John Ball, St Mary's priest, greets well all manner of men, and bids them in the name of the Trinity, Father, Son and Holy Ghost, to stand manfully together in truth, and help truth, and truth shall help you. Now pride is prized and covetousness thought wise, and lechery had no shame, and gluttony no blame. Envy reigns with treason, and sloth is high in season. God make the reckoning, for now is the time. Amen.

Thomas Walsingham was the most assiduous promoter of the idea that Ball was motivated by heresy, and had been influenced by contact with John Wycliffe or his followers. In his account of Ball's trial and death, he claimed that Ball had been preaching for more than twenty years, urging the withholding of the payment of tithes to priests who led unworthy lives. Ball was alleged to have preached in streets, market squares and in fields, like a medieval forerunner of the Presbyterian conventicles of the seventeenth century.

In spite of Walsingham's allegations, there is no evidence to connect Ball with the Lollard movement which, at this time, was still largely confined to Oxford University where Wycliffe was teaching. Indeed, the Leicester chronicler Henry Knighton, who was well informed about the doings of Wycliffe at nearby Lutterworth, where he was rector of the church in the period 1382–5, reversed the chain of influence, and identified Ball as the influence on Wycliffe. In fact, as Dobson states, Wycliffe, like Martin Luther, was no egalitarian in politics, and condemned the Great Rising in his later writings.[9]

The unusual blend of political levelling and evangelical egalitarianism in Ball's preaching and letters lends him a greater air of mystery than the tiler of Maidstone, and it is unsurprising that he has captured the imagination of religious and political radicals of later centuries.

Jack or 'John' Straw is the most problematic of all of the leaders of the Great Rising. In Thomas Walsingham's account he is the first of the rebel leaders to be mentioned, administering oaths to his followers that they adhere to 'King Richard and the Commons'. But after this initial reference Straw disappears from Walsingham's narrative until after Tyler's murder, when he is described as becoming the new leader. Clearly, Walsingham's narrative required a leader to replace Tyler, and this is accomplished by allowing Straw a dramatic gallows speech that, given his absence from much of the preceding narrative, seems highly incongruous. Straw's identity and role in the rising becomes even more problematic when we consider Knighton's description of the meeting between Richard II and the rebels, at Smithfield, on 15 June 1381: 'He (Richard II) was approached by their leader, Wat Tyler, who had now changed his name to Jack Straw'.[10]

Almost a century ago, F.W.D. Brie proposed that Wat Tyler and Jack Straw were, in fact, the same individual.[11] There were two principal foundations to Brie's case: the first that Tyler and Straw were seldom mentioned together, and the second that Straw is the sole leader mentioned by some of the later chronicles, and by Geoffrey Chaucer, in *The Nun's Priest's Tale*. Undoubtedly, Straw's identity is problematic, as he is not mentioned at all in the *Anonimalle Chronicle*. However, at no point does this source suggest that Tyler was a pseudonym, and both Walsingham and Froissart were explicitly clear that Straw and Tyler were separate individuals. If there is any scope for the conflation of identities, it is more likely to be between those of John Straw and John Wrawe, one of the best documented leaders of the East Anglian rising. John Wrawe was certainly real, as Walsingham's lengthy narrative of activities in Suffolk is corroborated by the records of his trial and execution.

Although Straw's identity as a real individual should be accepted, the evidence is far less convincing than that for Wat Tyler and John Ball, and historical constructions of his place in the Rising rest heavily on his popular 'canonisation' in the chap-books and pamphlet literature of later centuries. In addition to the trio of Tyler, Ball and Straw, there are others named by Walsingham about whom next to nothing is known, including John Kirkby, Alan Threder,

Thomas Scot and Ralph Rugg. It is very possible that these were aliases, and some of them may well have been executed under their real names in the aftermath of the Great Rising. The identities of the East Anglian rebels are far more secure, as they operated within their own localities, and they will be considered in chapter six.

Traditionally, the Great Rising of 1381 has been known as the Peasants' Revolt. Although hallowed by the frequency and duration of usage, the title is misleading in a number of ways. The words of the contemporary chroniclers have done little to clarify our understanding of the composition of the Rising. Knighton stressed the participation of apprentices, whose supposed predisposition to rioting was already established as a *cliché*, while for Walsingham serfs predominated among the rebels, whom he characterised as 'rustici' – country dwellers.[12]

But the records of trials in the aftermath of the revolt show that many social types, both urban and rural, participated in the disturbances of 1381.

Herbert Eiden's investigation into the composition of the rebel bands in Essex and Norfolk confirms the remarkable social breadth of the Rising. Of the 954 rebels from Essex whose names have survived, the occupations of 283 were recorded, and of these only *five* were un-free tenants. Most striking was the preponderance of Essex men who had served in the offices of village government; fifteen tax collectors, the same number of village constables and three bailiffs. Eiden noted a similar preponderance of local officers among the 1,214 Norfolk rebels that he identified: fourteen tax assessors, fifteen constables and five bailiffs.[13] Many of these men would have had a degree of literacy and numeracy, and would have been aware of the social composition of their locality. In fact, they were the ideal men to lead village revolts. But, opportunity alone cannot explain their participation. W. M. Ormrod has shown that, from the 1350s, the aggressive extension of royal government into the localities, through the commissions to enforce the Statute of Labourers, and later those to investigate Poll Tax evasion, destroyed the power of these village elites, who had hitherto been trusted to regulate much of daily life within their communities.[14] Moreover, these same gentry who enforced labour laws and taxation were also filling the benches as justices of the peace. This may help to explain why so much of the rural violence appeared to have been directed by richer villagers against their immediate social superiors, especially those who sat as JPs.

The role played by Londoners, both the enfranchised guildsmen, and the poorer labourers and artisans, cannot be exaggerated. The social and political hierarchies within the city were as firmly entrenched as those of the countryside. As Hilton has noted, only one-quarter of Londoners were full citizens, with the right to hold office, vote, and sit on juries.[15] The remainder had no permanent right of residence, and plied their trades casually, and at the sufferance of the authorities. However, this simple distinction between citizens and 'aliens' masks a much more elaborately stratified structure of competing social, political and commercial communities. The real nexus of power lay in the transactions and connections between the departments of royal administration, the royal household, the noble townhouses, the great merchants and victuallers, the brokers of capital and the law courts. The wealthiest of Londoners, such as the financier Richard Lyons, the draper John of Northampton, and the famous mercer and later mayor, Richard Whittington, operated in a world where the barriers of public and private interest were porous and ill-defined.

Geoffrey Chaucer, a vintner and customs official, lived at the very heart of this world, and his poetry evokes the ambition and status-consciousness of his own age. Trade and commerce in the city was systematically rigged for the benefit of entrenched monopolies, and internal protectionism was inherent to the structure of guilds and crafts. Therefore, it should not be surprising that many inhabitants of London felt that they had more in common with the labourers and artisans at their gates, than with their more privileged fellow denizens of the city.

But participation in the Rising was not confined to the poorer Londoners. The case of Paul Salisbury is illustrative of the ways that wealthier Londoners exploited the disturbances as a smokescreen for the pursuit of their own private grievances. Salisbury had designs on the property of an alderman, William Baret, against whom his deceased father, Sir Thomas Salisbury, had litigated unsuccessfully, with the result that he had been forced to quit his claim, and surrender a bond to the value of £200. On Friday 14 June, Salisbury and one of his servants, armed with swords and staves, went to the ward of St Mary Bothaw's, where they broke into Baret's house, and threw him, his wife and his servants out into the street 'making the said wife kneel a long time before him, and compelling them both to thank him for their long inhabiting of the said house and for their lives'. Salisbury and his men took care to seize the quitclaims and the bond of recognisance, and even made Baret swear to renounce his rights to the property. Buoyed by this success, Salisbury moved on to another property on Thames Street, belonging to Hugh Fastolf. Joan, Fastolf's wife, was assaulted, and, as in the previous attack, was forced to surrender deeds which had been granted by Sir Thomas Salisbury. In addition to an indenture by which Sir Thomas had conceded to Fastolf a £20 rent from the property, Paul Salisbury also made off with a cask of documents, and several pipes of wine and ale, with which he toasted the success of his expedition. As a final humiliation, he compelled Joan Fastolf to pay a penny's rent as an acknowledgement of his title to her husband's property. However, in spite of the brazen nature of his crimes, Paul Salisbury had a friend in high places – Sir Aubrey de Vere, chamberlain of the royal household (and uncle of the King's favourite, the Earl of Oxford) – and he received the King's pardon on 22 July 1381.[16]

This single case must stand for many less well recorded examples of larceny, crude opportunism and private score-settling. For all the power and breadth of vision underpinning the rebels' demands for economic emancipation, it was inevitable that their movement became a vehicle for personal aggrandisement unfettered by the restraints of legal and commercial process.

When Sir Charles Oman wrote *The Great Revolt of 1381* in 1906, one of the major historical questions was that of how the rebels had gained entry to the city. This question has since diminished in importance (in large part due to the research of Andrew Prescott) as it is now recognised that the majority of the rebels in London were themselves Londoners. Oman found the explanation for how tens of thousands of rebels (or so he believed) entered the city, through a series of trials that occurred in the mayoral courts during the aftermath of the Rising.

On 12 June a group of aldermen was sent by the mayor and corporation to Blackheath to deter the Kentish rebels from advancing on London. In the aftermath of the Rising, the failure of the deputation was attributed to deliberate acts of treason on the part of its members. John Horn was alleged to have not only disregarded his commission, but to have actively encouraged the rebels in their purpose. The gravity of the charges becomes clear when Horn was accused of dissuading the rebels from dispersing, and reassuring them that the Londoners would welcome their entry to the city 'as a lover his loved one'. With the rebel leaders accommodated for the night in his own house, Horn is alleged to have approached a city clerk called John Marchaunt, and, invoking the express command of the mayor, demanded that he be given a banner of the royal arms. Furnished with this banner, he rode to Blackheath, and, *en route*, met a royal messenger called John Blyton, who had been sent by the King to dissuade the rebels from entering the city. In the ensuing exchange, Horn refused to talk about his mission with Blyton, and, when he arrived at Blackheath, offered the rebels the strongest encouragement to enter the city. Thus, bearing the royal banner, Horn led the rebels to the city.

At least two aldermen were alleged to have been active in opening the gates of the city. William Tonge was charged with having opened the Aldgate, while Walter Sibley was alleged to have opened London Bridge. Even as the tide of the revolt turned against the rebels, Horn and Sibley supposedly locked the Aldgate to prevent men from crossing the Thames and coming to the King's aid, following the slaying of Wat Tyler on 15 June.

But, there is more to the case of the 'rebel aldermen' than meets the eye. The inquisitions of November 1381 were presided over by Walworth's successor as mayor, a draper called John of Northampton, who held office until October 1381. A highly abrasive figure, John of Northampton's mayoralty was dominated by fierce conflict with the victualling guilds, who were defending the monopoly on the sale of fish. In 1383 Northampton was succeeded in the mayoralty by his hated enemy, Sir Nicholas Brembre, and it was during his term that the supposed 'traitor-aldermen' were acquitted of the charge that had hung over them for two years.[17]

In 1940 Bertie Wilkinson highlighted considerable inconsistencies in the witness statements made against the aldermen, and observed that many of their alleged actions were impossible within the accepted chronology of the Great Rising. Perhaps the least credible charge related to the alleged efforts of Horn and Sibley to prevent the city of London from bringing aid to the King after Tyler's death at Smithfield. Even Tyler's most determined accomplices did not lift a hand to resist the royal reinforcements coming to Smithfield.[18] Therefore, the Great Rising of 1381 is a rare case in which the evidence of the chronicles can be used to correct errors in the judicial records.

Evidence for the fusion of 'local' and 'national' politics can also be found in England's 'second city' as York styled itself at this time. In 1380 the election to the mayoralty of John Gisburn had been accompanied by serious violence within York. This tension was exacerbated by the city's outrage and the escalating royal fiscal demands of the early years of Richard II's reign. In a mirror of the competition over the London mayoralty, Gisburn was followed in office in York by a rival from another political interest, Simon Quixley. Therefore, in the two greatest cities of the kingdom, internal politics reacted with the external forces of protest to produce widespread popular discontent.[19]

The Great Rising of 1381 remains, predominantly, a revolt of the poorer elements of rural and urban society against lordship and privilege, both seigniorial and commercial. The incineration of seigniorial records testifies to a popular hatred of noble lordship no less striking than that felt by the French peasantry in 1789. But, it is equally clear that the 1381 Rising was also used as a vehicle for the perpetuation of pre-existing conflicts, and commercial and jurisdictional rivalries, especially in urban communities. Many of the Londoners are likely to have rebelled for 'purely' political reasons – a hatred of John of Gaunt, resentment against the royal council's fiscal policies and a general resentment at poor and exploitative governance.

THE AIMS OF THE REBELS

One of the distinguishing characteristics of the Great Revolt of 1381 is the quantity of contemporary comment on the rebels' aims and objectives. Indeed, the pivotal moments of the revolt in London were the two occasions on which the rebel leaders presented their demands to the young Richard II. But, beyond this reportage, the chroniclers thickened their accounts with layers of their own interpretation and supposition. To borrow a phrase from the seventeenth century, the chroniclers of 1381 were witnessing a 'world turned upside down', and their sense of disorientation and horror may have acquired an added intensity from the ecclesiastical background of their writing.

The *Anonimalle Chronicle*, which has the most detailed account of the rebels' actions in London, records two sets of demands made by Tyler at his encounters with the King, at Mile End and Smithfield, on 14 and 15 June 1381. The fundamentals of this chronology have been questioned by modern historians, who suggest that Tyler had only one encounter with the King – that which ended with his death on 15 June.[20] Tyler's presence at the 14 June meeting is now widely doubted because there are no other sources to corroborate the *Anonimalle Chronicle's* account. But, given the inconsistencies of the sources on so many key points, this alone may not be sufficient evidence to disprove his presence. Rather, the strongest evidence to question Tyler's presence at the first encounter may be found in the inconsistencies between the two sets of demands.

The demands in the 14 June manifesto were for the punishment of traitors against the crown, the abolition of serfdom, a mandatory rent of 4d per acre of land, and freely negotiable contracts between masters and servants.[21] These demands represented the articulation of grievances that would have been commonly held, and are readily comprehensible in the context of the social and economic pressures of the preceding decades.

However, the second set of demands was an unusual and incongruous mix, some of which built upon those of the previous day, while others were extremely radical and entirely unprecedented. The first demand in the second manifesto (as reported in the *Anonimalle Chronicle*) was one that has caused debate among generations of historians – that 'there should be no law but the law of Winchester'. One explanation for this demand is that it refers to the rights that were popularly attributed to the tenants of the pre-Conquest crown estates. As has been shown, during 'The Great Rumour' of 1377 many villages had sought exemplifications from the *Domesday Book* to show that they had once formed part of the crown estate.[22] In 1110 an amended version of *Domesday* had been compiled at Winchester, and it seems possible that one of the vernacular terms for *Domesday* was the 'Book of Winchester'. However, doubt remains as to how common this usage was in popular references to *Domesday*.

Alternatively, the demand for the 'law of Winchester' has been interpreted as referring to the Statute of Winchester of 1285.[23] This statute was principally concerned with criminal law, and the preservation of order in local communities. How this related to the rebels' demands was not fully understood until Alan Harding high-lighted a section of the 1285 Statute:

> that every man have in his house arms for keeping the peace in accordance with the ancient assize;... that every man between fifteen years and sixty be assessed and sworn to arms according to the amount of his lands and chattels... And in each hundred and liberty let two constables be chosen to make the view of arms: and the aforesaid constables shall, when the justices assigned to this come to the district, present before them the defaults they have found in arms in watch-keeping and in highways...[24]

Harding identified this as a model for community self-regulation, allowing the commons arms for their own defence, and devolving to them responsibility for the policing and apprehension of criminals. In the post-Black Death environment when land-owning justices of the peace applied the Statute of Labourers to their own economic advantage, the 1285 legislation may well have been idealised by the poorer commons as the legacy of a more tolerant age. If this was what was meant by the demand for the 'law of Winchester' it would complement another of the demands of 15 June, for the abolition of all outlawry in legal process. As Harding has noted, this was no simplistic rejection of judicial authority, but rather a commonly felt resentment at the misuse of judicial commissions to uphold the private interests of powerful men.

While many of the 15 June demands built upon those of the previous day, the later sections were characterised by a departure into radical egalitarianism, founded upon the abolition of lordship and the division of property between all men. A whole new dimension was introduced in the attack on Church hierarchy, and ecclesiastical lordship. Wholesale disendowment of Church wealth was advocated, and the ecclesiastical estates, like those of the lords, were to be held in common. Only one bishop and one 'prelate' – a term that was left undefined – were to remain. But this radical levelling stopped at the person and dignity of the King, whose lordship, prerogative and estates were to remain untouched.[25]

Therefore, the distinctive character of some of the demands made on 15 June suggest that they may have well have had different authors from those of the previous day. Moreover, this is supported by the generally accepted chronology of the events of these two days. Richard's issuing of charters accepting the demands of 14 June caused a large proportion of the men of Essex and Hertfordshire to depart the capital that day. However, the Kentishmen were far from mollified by the royal undertakings, and they appear to have dominated the group that came to Smithfield – with Wat Tyler at their head.

Walsingham's account of Tyler's demands at Smithfield differs greatly, in that his central demand is the execution of all men practising the law. Given the savage violence that was meted out against men of law during the revolt (which will be considered in the following chapter), the demand is not inconsistent with the rebels' actions, but its absence from the manifestos in the well informed *Anonimalle Chronicle* suggests that it might not have been articulated at this meeting. However, Walsingham's account commands attention because it almost completely ignores the 14 June meeting (as he is more interested in the executions on Tower Hill) and does not focus on Tyler until the Smithfield encounter – when he briefly becomes the central protagonist.

Walsingham also found an explanation for the leaders' motives in a gallows-speech that he attributed to Jack Straw. Moved by the prospect of more merciful treatment at the hands of the Almighty, and at the prompting of the mayor, Straw admitted that the ultimate goal of the revolt was a holocaust of the propertied classes, including the King and the entire nobility. However, the mendicant friars would be spared, in order to ensure that the population would continue to receive the sacraments.[26] Given Walsingham's readiness to identify the friars as the principal cause of the entire

Rising, the bulk of the speech would appear to have been a fabrication, as it also contradicts the preservation of royal authority demanded by the rebels at Mile End and Smithfield.

But one perplexing feature of the speech that does demand further attention is the supposed plan for a federation of county-kingdoms, with Kent already reserved for Wat Tyler. During the revolt there were instances of popular regal usurpation, most notably those of Geoffrey Litster and Robert Westbrom, both of whom were called 'Kings of the Commons' of Norfolk at various times. In the aftermath of the revolt all of the recorded 'temporary kings' (to borrow a phrase from Frazer) appear to have been executed.[27] Although their other activities of leadership and instigation would certainly have been enough to merit capital sentences, their regal pretensions may well have distinguished them as being particularly worthy of execution.

The understanding of the rebels' aims of 1381 has been shaped almost entirely by the writings of their vociferous opponents, the Church chroniclers. Unlike the later rising of 1450, in which a substantial proportion of the political community, including the Duke of York, shared the Kentishmen's hatred for the leading courtiers, that of 1381 had no advocates within the institutions of government and administration. The voices of Thomas Walsingham, Henry Knighton and the other anonymous commentators comprise only one side of a dialogue, and so the modern understanding of the rebels' aims must remain painfully incomplete.

4

THE OUTBREAK:
10–13 JUNE

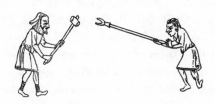

THE POLL TAX COMMISSIONS

In the late spring of 1381, those English counties closest to London were feeling the full force of the crown's efforts to secure full payment of the Third Poll Tax. If the Great Rising of 1381 can be said to have a single point of origin, then it must be the Essex town of Brentford and its adjacent villages.

The catalyst for the outbreak of violence in Essex was the arrival on 30 May of a royal commission to assess evasion of the Third Poll Tax. It was led by John Bampton, an MP and JP for the county, and also steward of the extensive estates of Eleanor Bohun, the wife of Thomas of Woodstock, Earl of Buckingham and youngest uncle of the King.[1] The commission began its work at Brentwood, by summoning the representatives of local towns and villages to account for the deficit in their payments, and, apparently, to levy further contributions. When confronted with further demands for payment, the representatives from the locality presented their receipts, which their assessors had been given at the time of the Third Poll Tax's collection. Threats made by the serjeants-at-arms who accompanied the commission backfired, and the townships of Fobbing, Corringham and Stanford-le-Hope dug in their heels and refused any further co-operation. At this point the sergeants-at-arms attempted the arrest of the representatives from the resisting towns, but they were driven from Brentwood, and John Bampton fled to London in fear for his life.[2]

Faced with the first overt act of resistance, the council resolved on further coercion, with the result that the Chief Justice of Common Pleas, Sir Robert Bealknap, was empowered to try the insurgents. However, the known records of Bealknap's movements conflict with the claims of the *Anonimalle Chronicle* that he had been sent to Brentwood at the head of a special commission. In fact, the Chief Justice is known to have been holding regular assizes in Essex and Hertfordshire, and there are no official records to show that he was driven away from Brentwood on 1 June, having attempted to indict rebellious men from the locality. But, regardless of the details of Bealknap's movements, it is clear that the crown's commissions of inquiry in Essex had sparked a full-scale popular revolt.

The speed with which the revolt spread was remarkable, and the *Anonimalle Chronicle* claimed that 50,000 men had risen by 2 June (although the actual number may well have been a fraction of this).[3] The first leader of the Essex men appears to have been one Thomas Baker of Fobbing, and he is credited with spreading the word of revolt to neighbouring villages and townships. In the judicial commission presided over by Chief Justice Tresilian at Chelmsford on 2 July 1381, Baker's name headed the list of men from the locality who were indicted for spreading the revolt.[4] In the aftermath of the Rising, John Geoffrey, a bailiff, was indicted for having ridden around the villages near Brentwood and Chelmsford, encouraging men to revolt. Geoffrey came from a class of literate and numerate local administrators, who would have been well-known faces in their communities. The organisational experience of such men may help to account for the speed which the Rising spread throughout Essex.[5]

The *Anonimalle Chronicle* suggested that a detachment of Essex rebels then marched south to join the Kentishmen at Dartford, and accompanied them to Rochester and Canterbury. But some rebels approached London from the north and the east, so it is likely that not all of those rebels who did proceed to London came via Kent. It is also important to emphasise that the revolt of the Essex men was not solely directed towards London, and perhaps the majority of them saw their own county as the locus for their protests.

While the chroniclers wrote of tens of thousands of men marching on London, Prescott's examination of the judicial records has led him to a dramatic re-assessment of the numbers involved in this phase of the revolt. Therefore, it would seem that the numbers marching to London may have been a few thousand at most, with the result that the Londoners themselves must have played a much greater role in the events in their city than has traditionally been assumed.[6]

The outbreak of violence in Essex had essentially been a reaction to the activities of the judicial commissions of the late spring of 1381. Contrastingly, the outbreak of violence in Kent appears to have fed upon more overtly 'political' factors touching on the relationship between the county and the royal court. Kent was distinguished by its close connections to the royal court, and many powerful men who had profited from crown service had invested in land in the county. Their property was a focus for attack in 1381, and again in 1450.

The spark that ignited the Kent rising appears to have been the disputed status of one Robert Belling, then dwelling in Gravesend. Belling was claimed as a serf by Sir Simon Burley, and he had sent two serjeants-at-arms to secure his arrest some time before 12 June. The *Anonimalle Chronicle* suggested that Burley went to apprehend the man himself, but it has been shown by Dobson that he was on a mission to Paris at this time.[7] Not only was Belling's arrest a strong-arm tactic, but it also represented a blatant abuse of Burley's court connections. After many years of service in the household of the King's father, Burley had also served as tutor to the young King, and had been made a Knight of the Garter in May of 1381.[8] He enjoyed a good rapport with his erstwhile tutee, to the extent that he was already in receipt of the royal largesse that would later make him something of a hate figure for the King's enemies, culminating in his eventual execution in May 1388.[9]

When confronted with the demands of the royal sergeants-at-arms, the bailiffs of Gravesend refused to surrender Belling, but hoped to negotiate some form of cash redemption that would enable him to buy out Burley's claims. But the *Anonimalle Chronicle* suggests that Burley would not accept less than £300 of silver to withdraw his claim – a sum that would have been beyond the means of all but the richest of men. Belling's inability to pay this sum resulted in his arrest by the sergeants, who removed him from Gravesend for imprisonment in Rochester Castle.

Just as the crown's judicial commission had been the spark of the Essex rising, the decision to indict the Kentishmen had a similar result. Popular hatred was particularly focused against John Legge, a royal sergeant who had been despatched with indictments for the trial of Kentishmen at an assize at Canterbury. The actions of the Kentish rebels suggests that, in addition to their outraged sense of natural justice at the treatment of Belling, they were possessed of a sense of county solidarity and corporate political responsibility. The *Anonimalle Chronicle* stresses that the Kentishmen 'although lacking a chief or leader' arranged to meet at Dartford, possibly on 5 June. Ever aware of their vulnerability to sea-borne attack at the hands of the French, they also ordained that all who lived within twelve leagues from the coast should remain at their homes.

Once assembled at Dartford, the Kentishmen marched on Maidstone, where they were alleged to have murdered a prosperous townsman, before proceeding to Rochester, which they reached on 6 June. Wisely, Sir John Newton, the constable of Rochester Castle, surrendered Robert Belling that same day, and he was borne back to Gravesend, triumphantly, by his rescuers.[10] Newton's decision to surrender Rochester Castle marked the beginning of a highly ambiguous role in the Rising. The chronicler Froissart claims that Newton was spared solely on the condition that he joined their ranks, and that this accounts for his presence during their march to London.[11]

After the fall of Rochester Castle the revolt in Kent reached a cross-roads. The men of Gravesend appear to have returned to their homes, but those of Maidstone and other towns pressed onwards. One band was led by Abel Ker of Erith, who attacked Lessness Abbey.[12] It is after the fall of Rochester Castle that the *Anonimalle Chronicle* makes its first reference to the most famous personality of the revolt – Wat Tyler. In spite of his posthumous fame, Tyler remains an elusive figure. The *Anonimalle Chronicle* is emphatic in locating his home town as Maidstone, while the jurors who sat on later inquisitions variously described him as being from Essex and Colchester. Brooks offers a sensible synthesis of this evidence by suggesting that he may well have originated in Colchester, but had resided for a time in Maidstone – although the reverse might be equally plausible.[13] The very fact of the jurors' confusion as to Tyler's origins suggest that his name may have been on the lips of many of the rebels from both counties. Indeed, from the first reference to Tyler the Kentish revolt appeared to be operating with a greater consciousness of the concurrent disturbances in Essex and elsewhere in England.

By now under Tyler's leadership, the Kentishmen marched on Canterbury. From the outset, the Kentish rebels appear to have been determined to present themselves as both Royalists and orthodox Catholics. When they assembled at Dartford, 'they said, among themselves, that were was more than one king, and they would neither suffer nor allow any king other than King Richard'. This may well have been a reference to John of Gaunt, and revealed much of the popular fears that his aspirations to secure the throne of Castile might be redirected closer to home. But, the Kentish rebels also appeared to have a strong hatred of the greatest power in the county, Archbishop Sudbury. The men of Kent not only endured Sudbury's taxes, but many were also tenants on the estates of Canterbury diocese – thereby magnifying their hatred of him.

According to the *Anonimalle Chronicle*, a band of at least 4,000 rebels reached the Cathedral on Monday 10 June. Entering the cathedral during the celebration of High Mass, the rebels demanded that the monks elect one of their number to replace Simon Sudbury 'for he who is now the Archbishop is a traitor who will be beheaded for his iniquity'.[14] Whether the monks complied with this request is not mentioned, but the mayor and burgesses of Canterbury wisely accommodated themselves to the rebels' wishes by swearing loyalty to 'King Richard and the loyal commons of England'. Ominously, 'traitors' were identified among the Canterbury townsmen, and they were summarily executed by the rebels.

As in Essex, those with political connections to the court and the royal council were particularly vulnerable to attack. Burning and ransacking were visited upon the buildings and livestock of Thomas Haseldene, controller of Gaunt's household, and also upon those of Thomas Orgrave, under-treasurer of England. William Septvans, sheriff of Kent, and a leading player in The Poll Tax enforcement commission of May 1381, was forced to surrender the court rolls from his manor of Milton, and these were duly burned.[15] Another victim of record-burning was Sir Nicholas Heryng, who suffered the loss of his rolls for his manors of North Cray and Foots Cray, and other documents stored at his house in Rochester. The rebels' hatred of Heryng was such that a group of them broke into Tonbridge Castle, in the belief that both he and John Bampton were hiding within.[16] Private score-settling appears to have been particularly rife in Kent, and this may in part have been due to the number of gentlemen in the county who had connections to the royal bureaucracy – upon which they would doubtless have traded to enhance their local standing and 'worship'. Sir Nicholas Heryng suffered the loss of two oxen, twenty-seven sheep and 482 wool-hides, together with goods and chattels worth £24, all stolen from his estates on Sheppey. Thomas Seintalbon, a prosperous man from Frendsbury, also suffered the ransacking of his house.[17] A.F. Butcher notes that William Medmenham suffered for taking his work home with him, as the rolls of the Office of the Receiver of Green Wax were burned in his house at Manston.[18]

The *Anonimalle Chronicle* claims that by this time the band of Kentish rebels had swollen to 60,000, although such figures always have to be treated with caution, and the real number is likely to have been considerably fewer. At this stage it would seem that Tyler and Ball were able to convince a band of the Kentishmen to broaden their objectives and march on London. Both Thomas Walsingham and the well-informed *Anonimalle Chronicle* identified the impetus for co-operation between the disparate rebel groups as coming from the Essex men, 'who sent several letters to Kent, Suffolk and Norfolk to ask them to rise with them'. If only a fraction of the Kentishmen marched on London with Tyler at their head, then his band could scarcely have numbered more than a few thousand, and perhaps many fewer than that.

Once the decision had been made to march on London, the rebels moved at considerable speed. Setting out from Canterbury on the morning of Tuesday 11 June, they reached Dartford the following day. Indeed, they overtook the King's mother, Princess Joan, who, learning of the Rising, had broken off her pilgrimage to the shrines of Kent, and was hurrying back to London. The rebels indulged in some ribald humour at the expense of the Princess and her ladies – regrettably the details of the exchanges have not survived.[19] On Wednesday 12 June a deputation from the London aldermen, together with Bishop Brinton of Rochester, met the Kentish rebels at Blackheath and urged them to disperse, but without any success, and Tyler's men continued towards the capital.

During the first days of the disturbances in Kent, the King had been at Windsor. News of the disturbances in Kent and Essex is likely to have reached him on the evening of Monday 10 June, as he set out for London by barge the following morning. During the King's journey to London, the *Anonimalle Chronicle* records that he sent messengers to seek out the rebels to determine their objectives and demands. Whether the impetus for communication came from the King or the rebels cannot be known, but it is likely that messages passed back and forth as the King approached London. While efforts were being made at Blackheath to discourage Tyler's men from a further advance on London, the King and the council were debating their own strategy in the Tower. By the morning of 13 June, it had become clear that the use of messengers to deter the rebel advance had failed, and it was decided that the King should make a personal appearance. The location for the meeting was Greenwich and, as before, the King travelled by barge. Although this was the standard mode of transportation, it also helped to preserve the King's security, as he could exit the Tower from a water gate. Escorted by four other barges, doubtless containing men-at-arms, the King and his council set out for Greenwich.

Whether concerned by the volatility of the crowds at Greenwich, or forewarned by some rumour of violence, or merely as an effort to preserve the royal dignity, the decision was taken that the King would remain on his barge, rather than venturing on to the river bank. The *Anonimalle Chronicle* suggested that the rebels were so enraged by the refusal of the King to meet them that they drew up a list of leading royal councillors whom they would execute. But, it is perhaps unlikely that the rebels necessarily expected a personal audience with Richard, and the composition of any death-list is unlikely to have been determined by such a refusal. Indeed, many of the names enumerated by the *Anonimalle Chronicle* were long established as hate figures for the Commons. In addition to those of John of Gaunt, Chancellor Sudbury and Treasurer Hales, the rebels also demanded the heads of two men at the heart of the royal governmental and financial machinery – John Fordham, keeper of the Privy Seal and Bishop-elect of Durham, and Sir Robert Plesington, Chief Baron of the Exchequer.[20]

The interconnection of local and national political grievances is apparent from the inclusion of several names – Sir Robert Bealknap and John Bampton, whose judicial inquiry had sparked the Essex revolt, and John Legge, the sergeant-at-arms who had been sent to Canterbury to indict the Kentishmen. Sir Ralph Ferrers' appearance on the list is suggestive of an enduring popular hatred against the men of the royal court. Ferrers had been one of the two knights who had invaded the sanctuary of Westminster Abbey in 1378, and had the blood of the fugitive squire Robert Hawley, as well as that of an entirely innocent sacristan, on his hands. Two years earlier he had been tried and acquitted in Parliament on charges of treasonable correspondence with France, but in spite of these notorious blemishes on his character, he remained a knight of the royal household.[21]

Unsurprisingly, Richard II refused to surrender the named men for summary justice, with the result that the rebels sent an unnamed yeoman to repeat the request for a personal interview with the King. The *Anonimalle Chronicle* claimed that the King wished to receive them, but that the Chancellor and Treasurer deterred him, and urged a postponement, until Monday 17 June, and the alternative location of Windsor Castle. This rather transparent effort to stall the rebels until forces could be arrayed at Windsor Castle did not yield any results, and no further reference was made to this proposed meeting.

The role of Sir John Newton in these negotiations has been subject to contrasting interpretations. Froissart locates his intervention to the period before the meeting at Greenwich, and credits him with encouraging the King to face his subjects, whereas according to the *Anonimalle Chronicle* he arrived at the end of the negotiations, and urged him to undertake the opposite course of action.[22] Regardless of what Newton really urged, the negotiations came to end without any resolution, and the King returned to the Tower.

On the morning of Thursday 13 June the Kentish rebels reached Southwark. By the later fourteenth century Southwark had become an important outpost of ecclesiastical and royal administration. The most significant buildings were the archiepiscopal manor of Lambeth, and the prison of the Marshalsea. Both buildings owed their situations to the peculiarities of the lay and ecclesiastical boundaries in London. The Thames marked both the boundary of the dioceses of London and Canterbury, and also the southern limit of the city. Lying just within the diocese of Canterbury, and occupied by the archbishops since 1196, Lambeth was a physical expression of the burgeoning secular and administrative demands on the holders of England's greatest ecclesiastical office. The growing frequency of Parliamentary sessions, and the increasingly institutionalised character of the royal council, demanded the Archbishop's presence in London for many months of the year. Simon Sudbury was the very personification of this interconnection of Church and state, as he held, simultaneously, the offices of Chancellor and Archbishop. Episcopal inns were becoming an increasingly prominent feature of the late medieval city, and the diocese of Winchester also had property in Southwark, while other bishops leased or owned inns on Fleet Street and the Strand.

The Marshalsea Prison was another feature of the jurisdictional peculiarities of later medieval London. For centuries the royal household had policed itself through the institution of the Court of the Verge (also known as the Court of the Marshal), the jurisdiction of which extended twelve miles around the person of the King, wherever he happened to be. As early as the thirteenth century, the city authorities had resented and contested any perceived extension of the Marshalsea's power at the expense of the Corporation.[23]

The increasing frequency of the King's presence in London in the fourteenth century had stimulated a growth in the business of the Court of the Verge.[24] By the reign of Richard II, much of the court's business concerned matters unrelated to the royal house-hold, brought by suitors anxious to short-circuit the slower processes of the Court of the Mayor and Corporation. Edward III himself had grown wise to the utility of this court, and had put up members of his own household to enter pleas to recover debts and punish infractions against royal privileges. The increasing volume of business coming under the court's competence is evident from the decision in 1373 to erect a building measuring 40 feet by 30 feet, on Southwark High Street, for the purpose of hearing pleas. However, its main purpose rapidly became that of a prison, reflected in its commonly used title of the Marshalsea. Ever jealous of their jurisdictional privileges, the Londoners voiced their hatred of the Marshalsea during the parliamentary attacks on the Court in 1376–7. In February 1377, Gaunt and his ally Henry, Lord Percy, the new marshal, were widely believed by the Londoners to have been plotting to extend the jurisdiction of the Verge at the expense of the Corporation. In 1376–7, Parliament had repeatedly peti-tioned for assurances from the crown that it would observe the city's privileges, and not to allow dishonest traders to evade the corporation's statutes by claiming trial in the Verge.[25] However, the crown's response, which was to restate the existing rights of the Verge, tended to increase rather than assuage the Londoner's fears.

Thus when the rebels reached Southwark, they were faced with buildings that were closely identified with John of Gaunt and Archbishop Sudbury, two of the most hated men in the kingdom.

The *Anonimalle Chronicle* described the first outbreak of violence in London:

> … the commons of Kent, to the great number of 60,000, arrived
> at Southwark where the Marshalsea was, and there they broke
> open and tore to the ground all of the buildings of the
> Marshalsea, and released from prison all the men held there for
> debt or felonies, and then they knocked down a handsome place

of John (*recte* Richard) Imworth, lately marshal of the Marshalsea, and keeper of the prisoners there, and all the buildings of the jurors and quest mongers around the Marshalsea were torn down that night.[26]

Similar violence was meted out at Lambeth:

Swooping upon the manor… they set fire to most of its abandoned contents, including books, clothes and linen; stove in wine barrels and drained them, pouring what wine was left on to the floor; banged together and smashed all the kitchenware; and all the while accompanied this behaviour, as if in self-congratulation of some praise-worthy feat, with shouts of 'A revel! A revel![27]

Both accounts are striking in their emphasis of the ferocity of the destruction wrought upon these buildings. But equally significant is the absence of reference to looting – a crime on which these ecclesiastical commentators would have pounced as evidence of the criminal traits of the rebels. Clearly, the leaders of the rebel bands were determined to preserve the 'political integrity' of their actions, and were doubtless sensitive to being labelled as robbers and criminals.

According to the *Anonimalle Chronicle*, the next target was a 'house of stews hard by London bridge, which was in the hands of Flemish prostitutes, and which they had leased from the mayor of London'. (Brothels were very common in Southwark in the middle ages, and one of the most famous houses of prostitutes was known as 'the Bishop of Winchester's geese' – after their landlord). But there is a problem with this chronology. The attackers of Lambeth are described as 'Essex men', and so would have had to have crossed the Thames from the north, through London. Given that this early in the revolt the men of Essex are unlikely to have traversed the city and crossed the Thames from the north bank, it would seem most likely that the group attacking Lambeth was comprised of

Kentishmen. If the Kentishmen had indeed attacked the Marshalsea first, they would have needed to perform a westward detour to Lambeth, and then follow the line of the Thames eastwards to London Bridge. A more logical route for the rebels would have been to attack Lambeth first, as the Marshalsea was on the route to London Bridge. Although the movements of the Kent rebels cannot be reconstructed with certainty, this would have been an easier journey for men who had marched all the way from Blackheath.

While the Kentishmen were ravaging Southwark, a separate crowd of Essex men had marched from Brentwood, and had encamped to the north of the city walls at Smithfield. Nearby was a tempting target, a complex of buildings owned by The Knights of St John. In the two centuries since its foundation, the Order of St John had acquired substantial assets in England, many of which had been gifted in order to fund its crusading activities, and its wealth had been further augmented in 1313 by its acquisition of the properties of the suppressed Order of the Temple, including the famous buildings of that name on Fleet Street. Sir Robert Hales had become Prior of the order in England in 1371, and he had become one of the rebels' chief hate figures. In February of 1381 he had been appointed Treasurer of England, and his personal identification with the aggressive methods of collection and recovery ensured that he was one of the prime targets of the rebels. His Essex manor of Cressing Temple had already been destroyed on 10 June.[28] The Hospitallers' property in London was acutely vulnerable – as both its headquarters at Clerkenwell and the Prior's manor at Highbury were easily accessible to the rebels.

The *Westminster Chronicle* captures something of the ferocity of the destruction wrought upon the properties of the Hospital:

> They made their way to the priory of St John at Clerkenwell and, killing everybody who offered opposition, burned down the entire structure, going on to consign to destruction in the ravening flames the manor of Highbury...

It is unlikely that the scale of the destruction inflicted at Clerkenwell, Highbury and Southwark could have been inflicted entirely by small bands of men from Essex and Kent. Many of the rebels in London were themselves Londoners, and so the view that most of the violence resulted from the 'invasion' of the city demands some revision. The role of the Londoners themselves becomes most apparent in the devastation that was wrought upon Fleet Street. The first building to be attacked there was the Fleet Prison, whose inmates, like those of the Marshalsea, were liberated. The neighbouring buildings of a chandler and a marshal caught the rebels' attention and were burned to the ground.

By the later fourteenth century Fleet Street had been long established as one of the most significant thoroughfares of the city. As the legal, financial and administrative institutions had become increasingly centralised in London, so the necessity grew for the political and ecclesiastical elite to maintain residences in the city, where they could reside during parliament, and entertain their companions. At this time, John Fordham, Bishop-elect of Durham and keeper of the Privy Seal, was residing at the inn of the Bishop of Chester, next to the church of St Mary le Strand. Revolt was thirsty work, and the rebels 'rolled barrels of wine out of the cellar and drank them, departing without doing further damage'. Given that the two other senior officers of state (the Chancellor and Treasurer) would be killed over the following days, Fordham had a very lucky escape.

Moving westwards along Fleet Street, the commons reached one of their main targets, the Temple. This complex of buildings had a double significance for the rebels, as it signified both the burgeoning power of the legal establishment, and the pervasive influence of the Order of St John, which owned the buildings. The attack on the Temple is notable because of the methodical nature of the rebels' attack – it had more of the character of a planned demolition than a frenzied ransacking. Trouble was taken to break open locked chests of documents in the Temple Church, while the rolls and books of the law students were collected from their individual cupboards, and burned in Fleet Street. Even the roof tiles were stripped individually.

The attack on the Temple was followed by the single most famous act of destruction performed during the Great Revolt. All of the contemporary writers commented on the grandeur of the Savoy, the London residence of the Duke of Lancaster. The Savoy had come into Gaunt's possession in 1360, together with the incomparably large landed inheritance of his father-in-law, Henry of Grosmont, Duke of Lancaster. Gaunt took considerable pride in his palace, and its gardens – complete with orchard and fishponds – which extended from the rear of the buildings down to the Thames. Tony Goodman has highlighted an instance in the 1370s when, doubtless at the prompting of his son, Edward III wrote to the Bishop of Carlisle, owner of an adjacent property, warning him to maintain his buildings lest the Savoy be left vulnerable to floodwater from the Thames.[29] Although no reliable image of the Savoy at the time has survived, the pen of Thomas Walsingham does something to conjure up a mental image – 'nothing anywhere in the kingdom was comparable in nobility or beauty'.[30] The scale of the destruction was made all the more terrible by the fact that, during the Duke's absence, the Savoy was being used as a store for all of his furniture and fixtures that were not in current use. The chronicler Henry Knighton recoiled at the destruction, as the Duke was the patron of his Abbey. Knighton was probably recalling a personal conversation when he remarked that:

> ... the keeper of the (Duke's) wardrobe himself said, on more than one occasion, and swore to it, that he believed that no prince in Christendom had a finer wardrobe and scarcely any could even match it. For, as he said, there were such quantities of vessels and silver plate, without counting the parcel-gilt and solid gold, that five carts would hardly suffice to carry them.[31]

Whatever their differences of interpretation, chronology, causation and blame, all of the chroniclers of the 1381 revolt were as one in their fascination at the destruction of the Savoy. In their accounts the chroniclers were anxious to recount every detail that they could gather, dwelling with horror on the destruction of individual items:

> And then at last they came to the Savoy, and, breaking open the gates, came into the place and, coming into the wardrobe, took all the torches that they could find and set alight all the very valuable cloths and coverlets and beds, and all the valuable head-boards, of which one, emblazoned with heraldic shields, was said to be worth a thousand marks, and all the napery and other goods that they could find, they carried them to the hall and torched them.

Both the well-placed Westminster chronicler and Thomas Walsingham observed that the destruction of the Duke's treasure was highly systematised. Gold and silver vessels and other precious objects were smashed with axes before being thrown into the sewers, or into the Thames itself.[32] It would seem that the rebels' motive was not to despoil the Duke to their own advantage, but, in the most literal sense, to deconstruct his possessions. This was manifest in the diligence with which his possessions were rendered valueless before their destruction or disposal:

> They tore the golden cloths and silk hangings to pieces and crushed them underfoot; they ground up jewels and other rings inlaid with precious stones in small mortars, so that they could never be used again.

Some of the violence done to the Duke's possessions had a distinctly ritualistic character:

In order not to pass by any opportunity of shaming the Duke completely, they seized one of his most precious vestments, which we call a 'jakke', and placed it on a lance to be used as a target for their arrows. And since they were unable to damage it sufficiently with their arrows, they took it down and tore it apart with their axes and swords.[33]

It might even be argued that the burning of the Savoy was an act of secular iconoclasm, through which the rebels sought to purify the city through the burning of the Duke's property. This quasi-puritanical disdain for the Duke's wealth – and in particular the precious vessels of his chapel – was complemented by a moral self-regulation. The *Westminster Chronicle* tells us:

A spectacle was to be seen there that is not familiar in our own day: with priceless objects in full view and under their hands as they assembled them, the yokel band did not dare to purloin any of the valuables since anybody caught in any act of theft was hauled away, without trial or judgement, to death by beheading.[34]

According to Knighton, one unfortunate looter was thrown into the flames, together with the piece of silverware which he had been found to be carrying, amid cries from the rebels that they were 'zealots for truth and justice, not thieves and robbers'. There were, of course, exceptions, and two Kentishmen – John Foxgone and Roger Plomer – were later indicted for stealing from the Savoy.[35]

At least two of the chroniclers claim that the Savoy consumed some of its own attackers. Knighton relates an anecdote that thirty-two men were slowly burnt alive in the ducal wine cellar, having drunk themselves into such a state of stupefaction that they were incapable of making their escape. A similar story was related in the *Anonimalle Chronicle*, which claimed that a group of rebels found three barrels of gunpowder, which, in the misapprehension that their contents were gold and silver, cast them upon the flames, with predictable results.[36]

For the chroniclers the burning of the Savoy was a morality tale upon which they freely grafted their own interpretations and judgements, and it says not a little about their neuroses over the spread of popular violence to their own comfortable monastic dwellings. Although the chroniclers tended to imply that the damage resulting from the burning of the Savoy was incalculable, the existence of detailed inventories enabled the Duke's officials to provide hard figures in their assessments of the losses. The goods in the chapel were estimated to have been worth £500 alone, while a pre-1381 inventory of the palace (excluding the physical fabric of the building), valued its contents at £10,000 – roughly equivalent to the Duke's gross annual income from his estates. But more illustrative of the destruction than these bald figures was the Duke's order of 1383 to sell 100s worth of the lead from the Savoy's roof, and to use the proceeds to pay for the costs of shipping the remainder to Hertford Castle, which was then undergoing renovation. After 1381 the Savoy was fit for little more than use as a warehouse, and, when he needed to be in London, the Duke rented properties from the Bishop of Ely and the Abbot of Westminster.[37] One indirect consequence of the destruction was a discontinuity in the ducal records, as much of his financial documentation was also lost.[38]

Had Gaunt been in the Savoy when the rebels attacked, would they have been content with his capture and delivery to the rebel leaders, and left the palace untouched? After all, the major governmental buildings at Westminster were left alone after the capture and execution of the Chancellor and Treasurer. Perhaps the attack on the Savoy was all the more intense precisely because the rebels knew that he was beyond their reach, and that its destruction represented an expiation of the anger that would otherwise have been spent in the butchering of its owner.

Undoubtedly Gaunt was 'the one that got away'. Had he been in London or its vicinity in June 1381, his life would have been in the gravest danger (although Gaunt was in the north of England, negotiating with the Scots, he was far from safe, and his experiences during the revolt will be discussed later). A rebel leadership that executed the Chancellor-Archbishop and the Treasurer would have had little compunction about despatching the deeply unpopular Duke. His vulnerability had been highlighted on the night of 20 February 1377, when he had narrowly escaped a lynching at the hands of a London mob, while dining in the house of his friend, the steward of the royal household, Sir John d'Ypres.

Inhabitants of the city played a leading role in the destruction of the Savoy, to the extent that one of the chroniclers even exculpated the Kentish rebels from the blame that was later attached to them. Perhaps Gaunt's decision not to rebuild the Savoy, or to acquire a new permanent residence, was motivated by a lingering fear that he might once again become a target for popular hatred.

On the following morning the group that had attacked the Savoy set out towards Westminster, where they burned the house of Sir John Butterwick, under-sheriff of Middlesex. They also broke open the gaol at Westminster and freed its inmates. But, satisfied with these achievements, they made no attempt on the complex of governmental and ecclesiastical buildings at Westminster, but returned to the city via Holborn, where they burned the tenements of one Simon Hosteler, and broke open the prison at Newgate. This was the fourth London prison to be broken during the Great Rising, which may suggest a degree of collusion between the rebels and the criminal underclass of the city.

The demolition of buildings for political reasons is a surprisingly rare occurrence in the later middle ages. The earlier Norman and Angevin kings had demolished unlicensed *adulterine* castles to cow dissident nobles, while the Tudors would allow decommissioned royal residences to decay and collapse as a means of saving money. Political demolition in western Europe would not come into its

own until the era of Cromwell and Richelieu, when the burgeoning state enforced its supremacy over the nobility, and other
sectional interests, by levelling the symbols of ancestral domination.

OUTSIDERS, ENEMIES AND VICTIMS

Although the revolt of 1381 was notable for attacks upon symbols
of royal, noble and ecclesiastical authority, violence was directed
'outwards' as much as it was 'upwards'. What informed the targeting of the rebels in 1381? The hatred of anyone connected to the
law was manifested in a wave of arson and murder. Although the
sacking of the Temple was the most conspicuous assault on the law,
many other attacks occurred throughout the areas of England
affected by the Great Rising, and there were some very notable
casualties. On Friday 14 June 1381 Sir John Cavendish, Chief Justice
of the King's Bench, chancellor of the University of Cambridge,
and a great man in East Anglian society, was apprehended taking
flight at Lakenheath in Suffolk, and beheaded. Justice Edmund
Walsingham met a similar fate in Cambridge. In his chronicle, John
Capgrave alleged that the rebels specifically hunted law students
with the intention of killing as many as they could find. In London,
one Roger Legett, a 'quest-monger', was dragged from the high
altar of St Martin's church, and beheaded at Cheapside.[39]

The victimisation of men of law is easily understood, given the
hatred of the commons for the statutes, assizes and commissions
that increasingly regulated their daily lives. There was also, however,
a more visceral and well-established pattern to the targeting of
unpopular groups during the revolt. During the twelfth and thirteenth centuries the periodic massacres of Jews had been a powerful evocation of the vulnerability of 'outsiders' at times of political
and social trauma. Paradoxically, Edward I's money-grubbing and
vindictive expulsion of England's Jews in 1290 may well have
spared their descendants from a far more brutal fate in 1381.

As in later centuries, marginal groups were acutely vulnerable to attack during periods of social and political unrest. As early as the thirteenth century, London already had well-established colonies of foreign merchants and traders, whose presence had helped to make it one of the most significant commercial capitals of Christendom. Gascons, Germans, Irish and Scots had long figured prominently in the commercial life of the city. The most successful of these aliens were admitted to citizenship, and some secured election as aldermen. Alien merchants also satisfied the crown's hunger for credit, especially at times of war.

During the reign of Edward III, Italians and Flemings had filled the vacuum left by the Jews in the commercial life of England. The outbreak of war with France in 1340 had stimulated a royal hunger for credit, and both the Lombards and Flemings were ideally placed to meet this demand. However, just as the Jews had suffered from the hatred and frustration of their debtors and commercial rivals, the Flemings, in particular, were resented for their success in the textile trade. As Caroline Barron has noted, in 1378 the free weavers of the city had petitioned against the commercial privileges enjoyed by the Flemings, and there can be little doubt that resentment against this group continued to fester throughout the early years of Richard II's reign.[40]

But hatred of the Flemings was not confined to the Londoners, and one of the first buildings which had been targeted by the Kentish rebels on 13 June was the brothel in Southwark. A Kentishman, Roger Boys, was indicted before Chief Justice Tresilian at Maidstone on 4–5 July 1381 for the murder of three Flemings in London.[41] This community's vulnerability was accentuated by the concentration of its settlement in the heart of the city, and their enemies had little difficulty in finding them on Friday 14 June. When the rebels came across a suspected Fleming, he was asked to say 'bread and cheese' and if he pronounced it 'Brote und Kase' his fate was sealed. The *Anonimalle Chronicle* tells us that a band of rebels came to a tenement near the church of

St Martin-in-Vintry, where they found thirty-five Flemings whom they beheaded in the street. Perhaps the most prominent of the Flemings to be murdered was Sir Richard Lyons, the merchant-financier who had famously been impeached in 1376 for his corrupt manipulation of royal debt. He met his end at Cheapside, which had become an unofficial place of execution during the Rising.

The massacre of the London Flemings was one of the darkest episodes of the Great Rising of 1381, and stands in contrast to the rebel leaders' proclaimed aims of economic emancipation and social levelling. Although motivated principally by commercial rivalry, this episode was compelling evidence that scores could be settled at the communal, no less than the individual, level and that perceptions of justice and vengeance were subject to the refracting prism of individual and collective prejudice. A figure of 140–160 was suggested by the *Anonimalle Chronicle* as the total number of individuals murdered in London during the Great Rising, but unfortunately this number is not broken down into categories of sex or social status.

THE REBELS AT THE TOWER

The failure of the negotiations held at Greenwich to deter the rebels from entering the city of London had shown the inability of the royal council, and of the young King, to uphold royal authority, and snatch the initiative from the rebels. Although driven largely by the necessity of self-preservation, the retreat to the Tower was an unmistakable symbol of the retreat of royalty to the circumference of its walls.

The rebels' two main targets, Archbishop Sudbury and Treasurer Hales, had reckoned that staying by the King's side would afford them greater protection than the hazards of flight from the city. Two other inmates of the Tower with much to fear were William

Appleton, a Franciscan friar and physician to John of Gaunt, and John Legge, the serjeant-at-law who had attempted to indict the Canterbury rebels. Present from among the King's own family circle were his mother Princess Joan, his two half-brothers Thomas and John Holand, his half-sister Joan Holand, Duchess of Brittany, and his cousin Henry, Earl of Derby, the son of John of Gaunt. Two senior earls were present – Warwick and Salisbury, as well as the teenage Robert de Vere, Earl of Oxford.

By the later fourteenth century the Tower of London had even greater perimeter defences than those extant today and, if defended, it would have presented a far from negligible challenge to a besieging army. But the quantity of manpower available to the defenders in June 1381 is a question that may never be resolved satisfactorily. Henry Knighton claimed that there were between 150–180 knights in the Tower, while Thomas Walsingham enlarged this force to 600 men-at-arms and 600 archers.[42] If either figure were accurate, it would have enabled the occupants of the Tower to have put up a very robust defence. But both figures need to be taken with much caution.

Not only was much of the kingdom's semi-professional soldiery committed to the garrisoning of English castles and bastions in France, but it is also highly unlikely that such a large force of experienced knights, men-at-arms and archers could have been assembled and brought to the Tower with such speed. Forces of this size were recruited through a sub-contracting system, requiring both time and large amounts of coinage for the payment of wages.

The Tower may well have had a skeleton garrison before the King's arrival, but it was unusual for a castle to be held by more than a handful of men other than at times of threatened invasion or civil war. There would have been knights and men-at-arms accompanying the King, but these are unlikely to have numbered more than a handful. Given that the main function of the Tower was as an arsenal, it certainly would not have been lacking in arms, armour and munitions. As castles were designed to maximise the domination of an area with the minimum number of men, the Tower should have been defensible with only a small force.

More telling, though, than the balance of forces were the factors that informed the decisions made by the King and the royal council. The decision to move to the Tower had brought an immediate improvement to the King's security, but it also seems to have paralysed the capacity of the royal council to recapture the initiative from the rebels. The *Anonimalle Chronicle* recorded how the King

> ...called all of the lords into a chamber of the Tower and demanded their counsel as to what he should do in this emergency; and none of them was able or willing to give his counsel.[43]

Thomas Walsingham was less circumspect in his words, and said of the armed men in the Tower that '...they appeared more like the dead than the living; for all their memory of past and glorious military deeds had been extinguished'.

When the rebels gathered outside the walls of the Tower on the night of 13 June, their position was considerably more powerful than it had been during their negotiations at Greenwich. Tower Hill was under their control, and they had already succeeded in destroying a consignment of supplies that had been sent to aid the royal party. The *Anonimalle Chronicle* claims that on the night of 13 June, the young King stood in a turret of the Tower and watched the flames from Southwark, Fleet Street, and, further to the north, Clerkenwell.[44] The rebels had not only shown determination and organisational skill, but it had also become clear that they commanded significant support from Londoners who were disaffected both with the politics of the court, and the dominant oligarchy. Above all, the events of 13 June had highlighted the shortcomings of the royal council's strategy, and the degree to which it had underestimated the strength and motivation of the rebels.

Although exercising a fascination for the contemporary chroniclers, the arson and destruction in London was, in fact, peripheral to the rebels' main objectives, which were the securing of royal concessions to their demands. Whatever Walsingham may claim about their supposedly regicidal instincts, the rebels of 1381, like the marchers on the St Petersburg Winter Palace in 1905, invested a profound faith in the capacity of the King to satisfy their demands. Richard II's personal response to that challenge to his kingship would shift the entire balance of political advantage within the capital, and result in one of the most memorable confrontations between a king and a commoner in British history.

5

THE KING AND
THE REBELS

Richard II's departure from the safety of the Tower, on the
morning of Friday 14 June 1381, was a considerable personal and
political gamble. At only fourteen years of age, Richard II was
taking upon his own shoulders a crisis that threatened to unravel
the fabric of state, Church and society. The image of Richard II
confronting Wat Tyler has acquired an iconic status, both through
its reproduction in printed versions of the contemporary chronicles, and as a tableau for the political interpretation of the Great
Rising by many generations of historians – from civil war
Royalists to nineteenth-century Marxists.

   In spite of the fame of the meetings between the rebels and the
King, their place in the broader context of the Great Rising
remains imperfectly understood. Some historians of the Great
Rising have questioned the extent to which Richard was master of
his own policy on the morning of 14 June, and have suggested that
his actions were largely governed by the advice of his councillors.[1]

Although the balance of influence and authority within the Tower can never be known for sure, there is no reason to suppose that the decision to confront the rebels did not originate with the King. Furthermore, it represented a reversal of the policy advocated by the royal councillors at Greenwich, which had failed to deter the invasion of London. Although the chronicler Henry Knighton argued that Richard went to Mile End with the intention of saving Sudbury and Hales, the political reality was that they had become a liability to the King, and his leaving them in the Tower could be seen as a means of distancing himself from them.[2] If the abandonment of Hales and Sudbury was a deliberate opening gambit by Richard to propitiate the rebels, then it was an indication of the desperate stakes facing the King as he set out for Mile End on the early morning of Friday 14 June.

THE MEETING AT MILE END

According to the *Anonimalle Chronicle*, the meeting at Mile End had been arranged for 'seven o'clock' on the morning of Friday 14 June. But, for all of its detail, this account should be treated with caution. The *Anonimalle Chronicle* assembles an impressive cast for this meeting – Richard is attended by his mother, his youngest uncle Thomas, Earl of Buckingham, and the Earls of Kent, Oxford and Warwick, while the rebels are led by Wat Tyler in person. However, the other chroniclers, including the well informed monk of Westminster, make no mention of Princess Joan and the Earls, and Tyler himself is completely absent from their accounts of the Mile End meeting.[3]

The *Anonimalle Chronicle's* account of both encounters between the King and the rebels is rich in quoted dialogue, but whether any of the rebels said 'Well met our lord King Richard, if it please you we do not want any king except yourself!' can never be known.[4] The substance of the rebel demands at this meeting was the surrender of 'traitors' for punishment, a general amnesty for their own actions, and a wholesale emancipation from all forms of serfdom and labour service. In the face of these demands, and the overwhelming strength of the rebels, the King had little choice but to appear to be as accommodating and complaisant as possible.

Thus, charters were issued and endorsed with the Great Seal of England, proclaiming the perpetual emancipation from serfdom of the people of the counties represented at Mile End. Messengers then rushed back to the respective counties with their charters.[5] Although each county received an individual charter, the texts were almost identical, and a copy of that sent to Hertfordshire came into the hands of Thomas Walsingham, the St Albans chronicler, and was included in his extensive description of the events in his own town:

> Richard, by the grace of God, King of England and France, and Lord of Ireland, greets all of his bailiffs and faithful subjects whom these letters reach. Know that, by our special grace, we manumit all of our lieges and individual subjects, and all others, of the county of Hertfordshire, and all of theirs whomsoever they may be, from all bondage, which we make quit by these present letters; and also that we pardon those same lieges and subjects, of all felonies, crimes, transgressions and extortions, committed by them, or by any of them, whatever they have done or perpetrated, and also of outlawry or judgements, which have been passed on them, or any of one of them, and which have or will be promulgated on this occasion; and we grant to all and any of them our entire peace. In witness whereof we have made these letters patent. Witnessed by myself at London, on the fifteenth day of June of our fourth year (1381).[6]

There is, however, a discrepancy in a draft of one of the charters, destined for the men of Somerset, which was discovered by Barbara Harvey in the muniments of Westminster Abbey. This charter is dated to 2 July 1381, by which time the suppression of the revolt in the south-eastern counties was well under way, and may have owed something to the distinct chronology of the disturbances affecting Bridgwater. It was not until Wednesday 19 June that Thomas Engilby attacked the hospital of St John at Bridgwater, with the intention of coercing the master to release certain bonds detailing the townsmen's obligations to him. Therefore, as late as 2 July, the Bridgwater townsmen were so convinced that the king would favour their cause, that they drew up a blank charter for him to authorise, clearly unaware that the violent suppression of the revolt was already well underway in Kent and Essex.[7]

One of the most important immediate consequences of the concession of the charters was to break up the rebels in London. In spite of their common aims, the rebels had at no point coalesced into a single force accepting the orders of a united leadership, and it is most likely that they remained a loose federation of county contingents even after their entry into the city. The bulk of the men of Essex and Hertfordshire appear to have accepted the charters at face value, and began to withdraw from London.[8] However, the Kentishmen were not so easily mollified, and their continued presence in the city had a decisive impact on the passage of events over the next forty-eight hours. As the absolute number of rebels in the city declined, so the Kentishmen came to exercise a disproportionately strong influence over the direction of the revolt. This may help to explain why their chief, Wat Tyler, had become the effective leader of the London revolt by the evening of Friday 14 June. Indeed, he may well have become leader by default, which would help to explain why his movements – which are scarcely recorded between 12–14 June, suddenly become so much easier to trace on the day of his death.

Had the Great Rising succeeded in effecting a major re-ordering of society, Friday 14 June 1381 would have stood as one of the most significant dates in British history, and would have enjoyed an importance comparable to Tsar Alexander II's liberation of the

Russian serfs on 3 March 1861 and Lincoln's emancipation of African-American slaves on 1 January 1863. Although Richard II's charters were cancelled within days of their issue, and formally rescinded in the Parliament that opened at Westminster in November 1381, the mere fact of their short-lived concession is a powerful testament to the ambitions of the rebel leaders, and their sense of the profound injustice of serfdom. This was the first occasion in the history of the British Isles that the people, *en masse*, acted directly to assert a commonly held conviction of their own liberty, and it would have profound reverberations for the politics of the seventeenth century, and later for the Chartist movement of the 1810s and 1820s.

Whereas the emancipation charter was repealed with little difficulty before its full effects could be felt, the question of punishment for 'traitors' was a more urgent matter, as the rebels were determined to have the heads of their enemies while they retained a decisive advantage. According to the *Anonimalle Chronicle*, the King responded – 'that the traitors should be delivered to his safekeeping, and that he would do justice to them as the law demanded'.[9] If this was indeed the King's answer, then it was a very diplomatic one, as he carefully avoided giving a mandate for lynch-law. In the event, the subtlety of the answer was lost on the rebels, as their actions would later show. However, regardless of whether or not Richard made the concession in good faith, his actions put him at the fulcrum of the revolt for the first time. Moreover, Richard II's cautious response to the cries for justice against the 'traitors' also revealed that he was well aware of the potential for his position to subside to that of a mere cipher for the rebel leaders. If the King's gambit of facing his people had bought him valuable time, the consequences for his ministers in the Tower were far bleaker.

The Executions at the Tower

From its earliest days the Great Rising of 1381 was characterised by violence. The high-minded aspirations to liberty expressed in the demands made at Mile End cannot be considered in isolation from the rebels' stated plans to liquidate royal councillors, central and local officials, and members of the judiciary associated with the collection and enforcement of the Poll Taxes. Moreover, once the rebels had entered London, darker forces of personal rivalry and commercial jealousy were unleashed. Although a number of local crown officers were murdered in the opening days of the revolt, the principal targets (with the exception of the fortunate Gaunt) sought security in the King's company, and this strategy brought them a measure of safety while Richard remained with them in the Tower. But, once Richard had set out for Mile End, those left behind were at the rebels' mercy.

Conflicting details are given for the chronology of the rebels' entry to the Tower. The *Anonimalle Chronicle* claimed that the entry was made by those men (supposedly led by Tyler) who had returned from meeting Richard at Mile End, but the other principal English sources attribute it to a separate rebel group which had remained behind. The chronology of both the attack on the tower and the subsequent executions remains hazy, and the *Westminster Chronicle*'s claim that the latter events occurred at eleven o'clock (four hours after the appointed time for the Mile End meeting) cannot be corroborated from any other sources.[10]

The most lengthy narrative of the events which followed at the Tower can be found in the account of Thomas Walsingham. However, the Scriptorium at St Albans scarcely afforded him a first-hand view of the proceedings, and it soon becomes clear that the main purpose of his narrative was to promote Archbishop Sudbury as a martyr, and to emphasise the sanctity that he exhibited during his 'passion'. However, Walsingham's account is also rich in incidental detail, and reflects a recurrent theme in his writings, a horror at the inversion of the established social hierarchy:

For who would ever have believed that such rustics, and most inferior ones at that, would dare (not in crowds but individually) to enter the chamber of the King and of his mother with their filthy sticks; and, undeterred by any of the soldiers, to stroke and lay their uncouth and sordid hands on the beards of several most noble knights. Moreover, they conversed familiarly with the soldiers, asking them to be faithful to the ribalds and friendly in the future... After the rebels had done all these things... they arrogantly lay and sat on the King's bed while joking, and several asked the King's mother to kiss them...'

In his account (perhaps drawn from the recollections of Robert de Namur who had been in London during the crucial period of rebel occupation) Jean Froissart added that the rebels did such damage to Princess Joan's bed that she fainted from the shock, and was subsequently allowed to leave by barge for the Great Wardrobe, about a mile upstream and to the west, on the city side of the Thames.

However, the robustly lascivious humour shown by the rebels towards Princess Joan and her daughter the Duchess of Brittany belied a far darker purpose to the invasion of the Tower. Sudbury, Hales and the other hunted men had no illusions about the rebels' designs upon them, and both Walsingham and the *Anonimalle Chronicle* state that, since the previous evening, they had been hearing Mass and confessing their sins. But Sudbury did not seem to be seeking martyrdom in the manner of Thomas Becket, as he made a bid to escape the Tower through its watergate, only to be foiled by the vigilance of a woman who noticed him.[12]

Although his subject was hardly a willing martyr, Thomas Walsingham did not let this get in the way of his gory narrative, which dwelt at length on the details of Sudbury's capture, words of admonition and piety which he exchanged with his executioners, and a beheading which required eight strokes of the axe – one of which was interrupted by his own exclamation 'this is the hand of God!' Walsingham's Sudbury displayed something of a vengeful streak in his posthumous career, and rather than forgiving his executioner, rendered him blind and insane. However, a man from Dover with a more reverential attitude to Sudbury's sanctity had his sight restored, and a pregnant woman who, having previously been unable to give birth, was delivered of male triplets after invoking his name.[13] The extent of her post-natal devotion to Sudbury is not recorded.

The other victims – Sir Robert Hales, John Legge, the ducal surgeon, Fr. William Appleton, and Richard Somenour of Stepney, a tax collector from Middlesex, were also despatched by beheading at the same spot on Tower Hill. The rebels celebrated their blood-letting with the display of the severed heads on poles, their eventual destination being London Bridge, where that of Archbishop Sudbury enjoyed pride of place, and sported a scarlet cap fixed by a nail through the skull.[14] His body was eventually returned to Canterbury, where it was interred south of the high altar of the cathedral, and a surviving Latin fragment of the tomb inscription describes him as having been 'martyred'.[15] More than two centuries after the murder of Archbishop Becket, Canterbury had acquired a new martyr, and this comparison was later drawn explicitly by the fifteenth-century poet, John Gower. However, the archbishop's head was not reunited with his torso, but taken back to his home town of Sudbury, where it remains to this day mummified in the crypt of the church of St Gregory.

One head that was missing from the grizzly display on London Bridge was that of Gaunt's son, the future King Henry IV. He had been in the Tower when Sudbury and Hales were taken, and, had he shared their fate, the subsequent history of later medieval England would have taken a very different course. The young Earl of Derby's life was saved by one John Ferrour, who was also in the Tower at the time of its invasion. The two men's paths crossed again, almost twenty years later, in the aftermath of the first revolt against King Henry IV in January 1400. A number of the leading rebels' accomplices had been brought to trial in Oxford Castle, and

Ferrour one of them. Recalling his earlier narrow escape of 1381, Henry spared Ferrour.[16]

Friday 14 June marked the high point of the rebels' fortunes in London. They had achieved their aims of killing the Chancellor and Treasurer, and had also spilt the blood of many more, including three of the hapless Flemings. Above all, they had gained the concession of the charters of emancipation which had been their central aim.

From the rebels' perspective, the King had capitulated – but in reality their personal loyalty to him, and dependence on his grace for the achievement of their aims, hobbled their freedom of action. Moreover, the total number of rebels in the city is likely to have dropped in the twenty-four hours following the meeting at Mile End. As many men returned to Essex and Hertfordshire, the Kentishmen and dissident Londoners were faced with a royal party which had survived the sack of the Tower and the execution of two of the great officers of state. King Richard had remained as a focus for loyalty among the surviving members of his household, and there were increasing signs that the mayor and corporation of London were prepared to come to the King's aid. But, most significantly of all, the opportunity to seize the King's person as a guarantee for his promises had now passed. The danger of this omission would become clear on the following day, when Richard II rode out to meet Wat Tyler at Smithfield.

The Meeting at Smithfield

The revolt in London climaxed in one of the most famous personal encounters in British history. And yet, for all of its notoriety, the encounter which culminated in the death of Wat Tyler remains subject to both the contrasting accounts of the contemporary chroniclers, and the similarly divergent interpretations of later historians.

Richard was better prepared for his second meeting than he had been for that of the previous day. Conscious of the vacuum left in his government by the execution of Archbishop Sudbury, he filled the office of Chancellor with the Earl of Arundel – a military man whose confidence, authority and maturity were well suited to this time of acute emergency. (Ironically, the relationship between the two men would become one of the most poisonous of the reign, and did not even end with the Earl's execution in 1397, as it was rumoured that his ghost haunted the King's dreams in his final months). The royal party had not returned to the Tower on the evening of Friday 14, perhaps deterred by the devastation and the grizzly scene of the executions, but instead had repaired to the Great Wardrobe, a large building at Blackfriars which contained the main financial office of the royal household. There, in the midst of the city, and surrounded by the rebels, the King spent what was doubtless a restless night.[17]

As Saturday 15 June dawned, Richard II readied himself for a second encounter with the rebels, which had been appointed for Smithfield, just to the north-west of the city. The King's most important preparation was spiritual, and, at three o'clock in the afternoon, he journeyed to Westminster Abbey. There he prayed at the shrine of his patron Saint, Edward, and made a donation at the altar, and is also reported to have confessed his sins to the anchorite at the Abbey.[18] The later successes of that day doubtless strength-ened Richard's devotion, and St Edward would remain his patron for the duration of his reign, an attachment expressed in 1395 when he impaled the royal arms with a blazon invented for the Confessor.

The King's enemies had also made the journey to Westminster, and it was in the Confessor's shrine that they found Richard Imworth, keeper of the now destroyed Marshalsea Prison, and a man renowned as a 'tormentor without pity'. As the tradition of sanctuary counted for little with the rebels, Imworth had resorted to wrapping his arms around the pillars of the shrine, from which he was bodily prized before making his journey to the execu-tioner's block at Cheapside. Another victim that day was a valet of John of Gaunt called John Greenfield, who paid the highest price for his supposed expression of sympathy for William Appleton and other men who had been executed the previous day. In the revolt's aftermath, an Essex man called John Sentlyne was indicted for Greenfield's beheading.[19]

From the moment that Richard set out from Westminster to Smithfield, the historian is heavily reliant on the account of the *Anonimalle Chronicle*. The sheer detail of its account, which included the words and gestures of the main protagonists, ensures that it remains central to any understanding of the passage of events that day. But, as Nigel Saul has cautioned, Thomas Walsingham, Jean Froissart, Henry Knighton and the monk of Westminster also detailed the famous encounter with Wat Tyler, and each differs in the order and unfolding of events.[20] Given the numbers who would have witnessed the encounter – at least 200 in the royal party, and many more among the rebels and the contingents of loyal Londoners – these differences are hardly surprising. Indeed, it is highly likely that individuals stationed at various points on Smithfield would have recorded distinct and conflicting impressions of the passage of events. However, regard-less of these differences, there is a skeleton outline of the actions of the main characters which commands broad acceptance. Some pre-arrangement of the movement of so many thousands of men would have been necessary, as the beginnings of the encounter were well ordered. Whether there was some communication between the King and the rebels is not known, but the royal group arrayed itself on the east side of the field, by St Bartholomew's priory, while Tyler's men kept to the west.

Jean Froissart, who may well have benefited from an eye-witness account of Robert de Namur, or some other French knight, is alone in suggesting that Tyler approached the King, unbidden, and without any summons from an intermediary. According to

Froissart, Tyler had a premeditated plan to seize the King and massacre his attendants, and that he had arranged to make a secret gesture to his followers to start the attack. Indeed, Froissart adds a nice vignette that Tyler had fitted out about sixty of his men in doublets acquired from a doublet maker called John Ticle, whom he had promised payment of thirty marks, once the day's business was accomplished.

But all of the other accounts credit Richard with the initiative for the face-to-face encounter, and make no reference to any supposed plot to seize the King. The *Anonimalle Chronicle* identified the man sent to summon Tyler as Mayor William Walworth, while Walsingham gave this role to Sir John Newton.[21] The *Anonimalle Chronicle's* description of Tyler's encounter with the King is so richly drawn that it merits quotation at length:

> And when he was summoned by the mayor in the name of 'Wat Tyler of Maidstone', he came to the King with a proud bearing, mounted on a little horse in full view of the commons and dismounted carrying a dagger in his hand, which he had taken from another man; and once he had got down from the horse, he took the King by the hand and, on half-bended knee, he shook him firmly and for a long time by the arm, saying to him 'Brother, be of good comfort and joyful, for in the next fortnight you will have forty thousand more of the commons than you have at the moment, and we shall be good companions'.[22]

This vivid and remarkable description of Tyler's words and gestures poses a number of questions. What was the meaning of Tyler's bizarre half kneeling motion, and his shaking of the King by the arm? Why did he address the King as 'brother' – and was it anything more than just arrogant over-familiarity? Finally, what did Tyler mean by the promise that the King would soon gain 40,000 companions from the commons, when it was already apparent that many rebels had already begun to leave the city?

There are no satisfactory answers to these questions, and it would seem that the young King was as bemused as anyone by Tyler's words, as all that he could say in reply was 'Why will you not go back to your own country?' This response angered Tyler, 'who replied with a great oath that neither he nor his companions would depart until they had their charter as they wanted it, according to certain points that they would demand, and he warned that the lords of the kingdom would repent it if they did not have the points that they demanded'.

Therefore, the *Anonimalle Chronicle's* account makes clear that Tyler and his fellows had not been satisfied with the general charters of manumission of the previous day, and that they had formulated their own more radical demands. As has been noted, Tyler demanded 'no law but the law of Winchester, that there should be no outlawry by any legal process, and that no lord should have any lordship, but that it should be held equally among all men, saving the lordship of the King'. In addition to this social and economic agenda, Tyler also demanded a levelling of the ecclesiastical hierarchy, the disendowment of the Church, and the division of its wealth between the common people. But, there is no satisfactory corroboration in any of the other sources for this radical programme.[23] Indeed, Walsingham outlined a different manifesto that centred on the murder of all men connected with the law.[24] The *Westminster Chronicle* – a reliable source that was seldom given to exaggeration or speculation – was far more prosaic, stating simply that Tyler had wanted 'a revised charter of liberty, since the one first granted by the King had not given satisfaction'.[25] The only detailed account of Richard's response was offered by the *Anonimalle Chronicle*, which claimed that he gave the calculating and ambiguous answer that Tyler 'could have all that he (Richard) could grant fairly, saving the regality of his crown…'.

All of the principal chronicles establish the cause of the violence that broke out during this interview as Wat Tyler's own behaviour. The *Westminster* and *Anonimalle Chronicles* concurred on his arrogant demeanour, and the latter has left us with a bold and engaging caricature:

> The said Wat Tyler demanded a jug of water for rinsing out his mouth because of the great heat that he felt, and then he proceeded to rinse out his mouth in a gross and disgusting way in front of the King and then he demanded a jug of ale, which he downed in a great mouthful.[26]

Tyler then remounted his horse, causing outrage among the King's attendants, who attempted to seize him. But Henry Knighton and Thomas Walsingham had a more elaborate and sinister explanation for the sudden outbreak of violence. In Knighton's account, Tyler is less of an uncouth buffoon than a genuinely threatening presence:

> He stood close to the King, speaking for the others, and carrying an unsheathed knife, of the kind people called a dagger, which he tossed from hand to hand as a child might play with it, and looked as though he might suddenly seize the opportunity to stab the King if he should refuse their requests... [27]

In Walsingham's account Tyler draws his dagger in anger at Sir John Newton, who had had the temerity to approach him on horse-back. Newton then his drew his own dagger – but then the King intervened and, wishing to avoid violence, ordered Newton to dismount. But Walsingham is alone in crediting Sir John Newton with a leading role in the encounter, and his narrative needs to be treated with some caution.

Caroline Barron has likened the scene of Tyler's death to the assassination of President John F. Kennedy, and to the extent that no definitive reconstruction can be synthesised from the many conflicting accounts, the parallel is quite fitting.[28] The *Anonimalle Chronicle* claimed that, just as Tyler was about to ride back to his men, one of the King's valets called him 'the single greatest thief and robber in all of Kent'. Tyler commanded the valet to come to him, but neither was willing to move, and there is some suggestion that Tyler feared some design against him. Tyler then ordered one of his attendants, who had been bearing a banner of St George, to dismount and behead the valet. However, the valet protested that he said nothing to merit his own death, and at this point Mayor Walworth intervened to reason with Tyler.

All of the main sources concur that Tyler then rushed towards the King and Mayor Walworth. At this point it would seem that a number of armed royal attendants, who had been holding back, came to the King's side. Walworth (or Richard himself) then ordered Tyler's arrest, causing him to strike out at the mayor with his dagger. According to the *Westminster Chronicle* the blow missed, while the *Anonimalle Chronicle* argued that it struck home, but that Walworth was protected from its full force by concealed armour that he was wearing.[29]

Any frame-by-frame reconstruction of Tyler's death is complicated by the increasing speed of events and the variety of the accounts. But, all of the sources concur that Mayor Walworth then struck Tyler at least one disabling dagger blow – whether it be on the head, through the neck, or through the torso. But the fatal blows were struck by a royal esquire, Ralph Standish, who ran him through, repeatedly, with a sword. It would seem, though, that Tyler still had the strength to remount his horse, and he managed to ride a few paces towards his followers, before collapsing again.[30] According to the *Anonimalle Chronicle*, Tyler was then dragged by his companions to St Bartholomew's Hospital, where he was put to bed in the master's room. But he did not remain there long, as Walworth's men came to track him down, and he was soon dragged back to Smithfield, where he was beheaded. But, given the severity of the wounds that he had already sustained, Tyler may well have been dead by the time that he was brought back to Smithfield. In a grisly display, Tyler's severed head was placed on a pole, and paraded before the rebels. Whether the sight of their leader's head reduced the rebels to imploring for the King's mercy cannot be known, but it seems clear that Tyler's death had seized the initiative from the rebels, and left them unsure of their next actions. Significantly, none of the rebels was able or willing to take Tyler's place, and rally them against the loyal Londoners under Walworth's leadership.

The quick reactions of Walworth and Standish may well have saved the King's life, but it was Richard himself who appreciated the broader dangers of the situation. At the time of his stabbing, Tyler had exhorted his followers to avenge him, and one of the chroniclers claimed that the rebels had begun to draw their bowstrings. Showing remarkable courage, Richard rode out towards the rebels, and urged them to meet him at Clerkenwell fields, to the north of Smithfield. Richard was now well guarded by a group of men-at-arms, led by the veteran knights Sir Robert Knolles and the Gascon Sir Perducas d'Albret.[31]

But for the young King's grasp of the situation, Smithfield could have degenerated into a bloodbath, especially if a volley of arrows had been unleashed by Tyler's followers. By encouraging the rebels to move northwards to Clerkenwell, Richard was drawing them away from the city, thereby allowing Mayor Walworth and his men the opportunity to re-establish some control. Richard was not slow in acknowledging the actions of the men who had stood by him when he confronted Tyler. The most famous of these was William Walworth who, in spite of his protests that his trade as a fishmonger disqualified him from such an honour, was dubbed as a knight that same afternoon. Other Londoners similarly honoured were the grocers, John Philpot and Nicholas Brembre, and the goldsmiths Robert Launde and Nicholas Twyford. This sudden expression of royal favour also showed the King's consciousness of the need to retain the affection and loyalty of these men, and the powerful interest groups they represented, while restoring order to the city.

Inevitably, the sudden and violent circumstances of Tyler's death has led to speculation about whether the scuffle detailed by the chroniclers was the full story. Recently, Nigel Saul has renewed this debate, by considering the actions of those outside the immediate group where the scuffle involving Tyler and Walworth broke out. Saul highlights the speed with which the loyal Londoners led by Sir Robert Knolles came to the King's aid at Smithfield, and also the intelligence with which the royal party had exploited the topography of Smithfield to prevent the rebels gaining a clear view of what was happening to their leader. Had Walworth been briefed in advance to gain the support of the men of the city?[32] It is difficult to determine whether this evidence is sufficient to make a reasonable case that Tyler had been 'set up' by the King and mayor.

One argument against the 'set up' theory is the vulnerability of the King throughout the encounter. Had the entire meeting been geared towards seizing Tyler, why was Richard placed in such a dangerous position throughout the episode? It is highly unlikely that his speech to the rebels in the aftermath of Tyler's death was pre-planned, especially as one well-aimed arrow would have been enough to make a disaster of the day. The case remains open on how the royal forces managed to turn the tables so quickly on the rebels – and the swift arrival of loyal men from the city may well have been unconnected to a premeditated plot against Tyler.

What is certain is the remarkable totality and speed of the collapse of resistance in London in the aftermath of Tyler's death. Indeed, it would seem that the entire movement, and not just its leader, had been beheaded. Whereas in Norfolk the Bishop of Norwich would have to defeat the rebels, in London their resistance dissolved in the face of royal authority. Whether any inferences can be drawn from this about the nature of Tyler's leadership remains open to question. Wat Tyler had never been the sole leader of all of the rebels, who appear to have remained in discrete 'county' groupings even after their entry into London. But, as the evidence from St Albans shows, his fame had spread rapidly, and he may well have been regarded as the revolt's *de facto* leader from provincial rebels seeking direction from London. Moreover, it was only with Tyler's death that the crown and the city authorities enjoyed the upper-hand in London.

The mystery about the nature of Tyler's role in London is accentuated by the irregular and infrequent references to him in the chronicles before the day of his fatal encounter with Richard. Even more than the sack of the Savoy, the encounter between the boy King and the rebel from Maidstone has become the single image from 1381 that is most firmly embedded in the common political memory. Indeed, their supposed dialogue might be regarded as a symbolic personification of the broader political and social factors underpinning the entire Rising.

But, for all of its impact on the revolt in London, Tyler's death had few immediate or direct effects in the other parts of England where locally based risings were still to reach their peak of activity. In the following chapter, the focus will shift away from London to consider events in Hertfordshire, Leicestershire, East Anglia and other parts of England affected by popular insurrection in June and July 1381.

6

THE COUNTY RISINGS

Although the historical construction of the Great Rising, and its place in English history, have been dominated by the events in London, which were played out in locations and by characters whose names have a resonance to this day, many other parts of England also witnessed great disturbances, which were often of longer duration than those affecting the capital. In East Anglia in particular, the patterns of violence and repression differed considerably from those in London.

Nicholas Brooks has cautioned against excessive generalisation when considering the causes of the Great Rising. The chronology and chain of causation in the risings outside London differs in many respects from the invasion of the city by the men of Essex and Kent.[1] But, to extend Brooks' argument, further differentiation is necessary between different types of rising outside London. Events in Derbyshire in the days following the collapse of the London rising confirmed the extent to which local politics had become enmeshed with those of the broader insurrection. On 18 June 1381 John Tailor of Morley, Henry Vepount and John Derby broke into Horston Castle, a crown property leased by a prominent county gentleman, Sir Robert Swillington, who was closely associated with John of Gaunt. Although the intruders bore the banner of St George, this was – both literally and metaphorically – a flag of convenience. David Crook has shown that their attack on Horston Castle was the latest act of a long-running local feud between the tenants of a powerful local family, the Stathums of Morley and those of John of Gaunt.[2] There were several urban disturbances coinciding with the Great Rising which were almost entirely caused by internal political rivalries, and had little connection to the broader movement against royal taxation, seigniorial oppression and partial justice.

Perhaps the most significant of these was the urban rising in York, which centred on the controversial mayoralty of John Gisburn, who had defeated his rival Simon Quixley in the election of 1380.[3] Although a fascinating example of internal urban conflict, it is not central to the story of the Great Rising. Similarly, the disturbances in the town of Bridgwater revolved entirely around the private ambitions of a handful of men against the Augustinian Hospital of St John, and unlike the rising in St Albans (where the rebels appealed for Tyler's leadership), there was little sense that it fitted into a broader movement.[4]

Consequently, this chapter will focus on those localities where the demands of the rebels were comprehensible within the broader Rising, and also where their actions revealed a consciousness of events outside their locality. Events in St Albans and Leicester will be considered first, as the occurences in these towns were fairly self-contained. By far the most significant events outside London occurred in East Anglia. The Rising in Suffolk and Cambridgeshire will be considered next, followed by that in Norfolk. This chapter has the twin intentions of examining the various forms of rising in the towns and counties, while also attempting to establish their significance within the context of the broader narrative of 1381.

THE REVOLT IN ST ALBANS

The uprising in St Albans is recorded in the single most detailed narrative for the Great Rising in any English town outside London. But events in the town are viewed entirely through the eyes of a single – and highly partial – witness. Thomas Walsingham, monk and precentor of St Albans, found the events there horrifying and compelling in equal measure.[5] But Walsingham's account remains essential due to his access to copies of the charters extorted from the Abbey and King Richard during the Rising.

Events in St Albans can only be understood in the context of more than a century and a half of struggle between the townsmen and the Abbey. As early as 1274, the townsmen of St Albans had attempted to throw off the bonds that had subordinated them to the Abbey.[6] Indeed, the events of 1381 are almost a mirror of those of 1326–7, when the townsmen had capitalised on the vacuum of royal authority to revolt against Abbot Hugh Eversdone. Although the origins of the dispute had lain in the Abbey's prosecution, in 1314, of a townsman called Robert Limbury for the use of a hand-mill, this case symbolised wider grievances over boundaries, common land, and rights of warren and fishing.[7] The townsmen's demands were encapsulated in their claim to be recognised as the citizens of a borough, and not villeins of the Abbot's manor. On 11 March 1327, after months of disturbances, the crown formally recognised that St Albans was a borough.[8] However these privileges were short-lived, and after determined lobbying of the new King Edward III by Abbot Richard Wallingford, the townsmen lost their burghal status in September 1331.[9]

The events of these years left bitter memories and profound mutual suspicion. The monks, no less than the townsmen, drew upon the town's recent history for the validation of their position. On 13 May 1328, Walter Amundesham, Abbot Richard Wallingford's esquire and marshal, had become involved in an affray when trying to serve a summons on a prominent townsman, John

Taverner, on charges of adultery. In the ensuing struggle Amundesham was slain, although not before he had despatched the man he had been sent to arrest.[10] In the Abbey's *Book of Benefactors*, which Thomas Walsingham himself compiled in 1380, Walter Amundesham ('a faithful minister of the church') was commemorated as having been 'murdered' by the villeins.[11] With this stark polarisation of collective memory, St Albans had the ideal composition of combustible materials for a sudden and violent explosion of urban protest. History, it seems, was about to repeat itself.

In spite of the great detail in his account, Thomas Walsingham is unable to say how news of events in London reached St Albans. However, it would seem that the news must have arrived in the late afternoon or evening of Corpus Christi day, Thursday 13 June, as a group of townsmen marched to the Abbey in the first few minutes of the following day. The demands that they made of Abbot Thomas de la Mare are unrecorded, but the following morning the St Albans townsmen resolved on marching to London, with the intention of securing their liberty as burgesses. Abbot Thomas and his monks had resolved on the same course of action, but they intended to contact the King, and re-assure him of their loyalty – presumably in the hope of some royal assistance. However, they also had news that the Earl of Warwick would be passing through Barnet *en route* to London, and they hoped to make contact with him there, in the hope that he would represent their case to the King.[12]

Earl Thomas and Countess Margaret Ferrers were two of the Abbey's most prominent patrons, and had made donations towards the repair of the refectory in the 1370s. Their devotion to St Albans was rewarded by admission to the Abbey's confraternity in 1377. On the day of their admission, the Earl and Countess had been attended by some of their leading retainers, including Sir Nicholas Lilling and Sir William Bagot, and it is clear that they encouraged members of the Beauchamp affinity to share in their patronage of St Albans.[13]

Once they had met the Earl, who assured them that he would bear their message to the King, the Abbot's men resumed their journey to London. Their first impression of the London rising was a dramatic one, as the road to the city passed the blazing complex of buildings owned by the Knights of St John at Highbury, and it was there that they claimed to have seen Jack Straw receiving oaths of loyalty to Richard II from the rebels.[14] However, due to the delay experienced by the Abbot's men while waiting for the Earl of Warwick at Barnet, the St Albans townsmen had arrived in London first, and had gathered at the church of St Mary Arches.

According to Walsingham, it was there that they resolved on a manifesto which included revised boundaries, the right to pasture cattle, to hunt and to fish, and also to erect hand-mills for the grinding of their own corn. Above all they wanted their town to be exempt from the jurisdiction of the Abbey's bailiff – which, essentially, was a *de facto* recognition of their right to self-government. But, what is most significant of all is the claim by Walsingham that they looked to Wat Tyler, 'leader of the ribalds and rustics of Kent' for sanction for their deeds.[15] However, the rebels also hedged their bets by drawing up a letter seeking confirmation of their pretended liberties from the King as well. Therefore, the St Albans men appeared to have envisaged two parallel and distinct authorities operating in London on 14 June – the *de iure* royal grace of Richard II, which had the capacity to deliver the written emancipation that they required, and the *de facto* power of Tyler and his men, to enforce their liberties against the Abbey of St Albans.

The man entrusted with both tasks was one William Grindecobbe, for whom Walsingham reserved a special hatred, as he had supposedly owed his education to the St Albans monks. Grindecobbe joined the representatives of the other counties and towns who had come to Mile End on 14 June and, on bended knee, received the emancipation charter from Richard II. His next visit was to Wat Tyler, before whom he pleaded his case against

St Albans Abbey. Walsingham seems to imply that Grindecobbe was not alone in seeking Tyler's approval for his men's actions, and this may give a hint of the nature of the authority enjoyed by the leader of the Kentishmen.[16]

In one respect the St Albans men were following a well-worn path, as in February 1327 their ancestors had marched to St Paul's, where they received a charter of liberties issued in the name of Edward III. Although Walsingham does not specify that Grindecobbe and his fellows were consciously imitating their forebears, it might well be supposed that a store of common memory informed the political choices that they made. However, whereas Edward III's power had been that of the inherited prerogatives of kingship, what kind of authority was Tyler credited with in 1381? Perhaps it was the common perception of Tyler's personal pre-eminence that drew county rebels to seek his power, or that his occupation of London itself conferred an intangible authority.

After a lordly show of reluctance, Tyler agreed to send a large number of his men to St Albans to enforce the newly gained rights of the town, should the monks attempt any resistance. But Tyler's price was high, and he is supposed to have commanded absolute obedience to his word, and made the men of St Albans swear an oath to this effect. The reciprocal nature of this encounter between Tyler and the St Albans rebels is notable, as it raises further questions about the dynamics of the relationship between the city and the counties during the Great Rising. Tyler's usurpation of the royal prerogatives of grace and the use of military force further emphasises the personal nature of his leadership.[17]

Satisfied with their charter, and the verbal assurance of Tyler's favour, Grindecobbe and his fellows set out for home. However, this time the monks were determined to be one step ahead, and they had already sent a messenger to St Albans conveying the news of the royal charter, and of the executions of Sudbury and Hales. This description was enough to cause the Prior, four of his fellow monks and a group of townsmen closely associated with the Abbey to flee St Albans. They did not stop until they had reached the Abbey's Northumbrian daughter-house of Tynemouth, putting 300 miles between themselves and their enemies.

When Grindecobbe returned to St Albans his agenda differed little from that of the men who had risen against the Abbey in 1326. The townsmen immediately set about taking direct action on disputed boundaries and other areas where the Abbey had supposedly encroached on common lands. The task of tearing down fences and sheep-folds was too great for the townsmen alone, and they summoned assistance from other villages and hamlets that were under the Abbey's lordship. Walsingham claimed that the St Albans men were learning lessons taught them by Wat Tyler, but there is nothing particularly novel in their efforts to increase their strength through the support of their neighbours.

One of the more notable aspects of the St Albans revolt was the role that ritual played in the overturning of the pre-existing order. No less than the men who sacked the Savoy, the St Albans townsmen used a symbolic vocabulary to celebrate their successes. Some of their most enduring grievances had centred on the rights of free-warren (i.e. the trapping of rabbits) and pasture, which they claimed to enjoy in common. They marked their new-found liberty by attaching a live rabbit to the pillory in St Albans town – a gesture which at once celebrated their right of free-warren while also repudiating the Abbot's judicial authority.[18]

But, the St Albans townsmen went beyond the mere rejection of their erstwhile lord, and they began to usurp his authority. The Abbey's gaol was broken open, and they released its occupants, on the condition that they swore to be loyal to the town and community. However, one unfortunate judged to be worthy of death was immediately executed outside the Abbey gates, and his head displayed on a pole 'with much shouting, which they had learned at the time of Archbishop Sudbury's execution'. Clearly Walsingham regarded the Londoners as having exercised a malign influence on the men of St Albans.[19]

So far the Abbot (unlike the Prior, who had fled) had sat out the disturbances and had avoided making any moves to either resist or placate the rebels. But his situation became more complicated upon the arrival of one Richard Wallingford (not to be confused with the earlier abbot of the same name who had defeated the townsmen in the 1330s), a townsman of St Albans who had remained in London on Grindecobbe's orders to secure the royal letters confirming their demands. The crushing humiliation of Abbot de la Mare can only be imagined when he read the letter:

> At the petition of our beloved lieges of the town of St Albans, we do will and command that certain charters, being in your keeping, made by our progenitor, King Henry (II) unto the burgesses and good people of the said town, of common, of pasture and of fishery and other certain rights, expressed in the same charters, as they say, you do cause to be delivered unto the said burgesses and good folks that which law and right demands; do that henceforth they should have no grounds for making pleas to us on this matter. Given under our signet at London, 15 June in the fourth year of our reign.

However, the men of St Albans were mindful of the circularity of history in their town. In 1326 they had exulted at throwing off the Abbey's lordship, only to endure the humiliation of its re-imposition. Therefore, their next action was to demand the surrender of all deeds and documents relating to the Abbey's over-lordship of the town, which were duly surrendered and burned at the Market Cross. Just as the attaching of the rabbit to the pillory had ritualised the claim of the townsmen to free-warren, so the burning of the records in the heart of the town's commercial centre lent a highly symbolic character to their emancipation.

But the townsmen's sense of history was not just rooted in a desire to erase the Abbey's power. They also believed that charters granted by Offa, founder of the Abbey, and by Henry II, existed in the St Albans chartulary to prove their burghal status. Although the Abbey certainly possessed a large collection of charters, it is unlikely that any contained the proof that the townsmen were seeking. In the case of the supposed charter of Offa, Abbot de la Mare repeatedly denied its existence.

The insistence of the townsmen on this point is illustrative of their inheritance of an imaginary chartulary of common memory. But their reversal of history also found more tangible expressions. When Abbot Wallingford had overthrown their short-lived liberty in 1330, he had confiscated more than 80 stones from hand-mills, and these he had used to pave the Abbey cloister. The mill-stones were now extracted with various implements and taken away – although whether they were still fit for grinding cereals is not known.[20]

To cap their successes, the townsmen demanded a charter of liberties from the Abbot himself, confirming the letter sent to them by Richard II. At this point Abbot de la Mare decided to stall for more time, causing the townsmen to threaten to demolish the Great Gate. Wisely, the Abbot bribed them with copious amounts of bread and ale to reconsider their plans.[21] However, the more that the Abbot stalled over granting the townsmen a charter, the angrier they became. Perhaps the townsmen were also beginning to fear that events in London were not going to plan, and that the promised assistance and leadership from Wat Tyler would not materialise. Although Walsingham makes no mention of it, rumours of Tyler's death may already have reached Hertfordshire.

Fearing that a relief force would soon come to support the Abbey, the townsmen took up defensive positions on the outskirts of St Albans. Any men suspected of entering or leaving the town with the intention of bringing succour to the Abbey were threatened with execution. They also proclaimed that any men who were owed money by the Abbey should come to St Albans the following day, and that the townsmen would ensure that they had satisfaction for their debts. Men from the locality were not slow in coming forward to take up this offer, to the horror of Thomas Walsingham. By 16 June the events in St Albans were lagging behind those in London, and the townsmen's triumph would be short-lived. At some point on 16 or 17 June Richard II's order countermanding the charter given to Grindecobbe and Wallingford reached St Albans. The order was dated to the same day as the first charter – 15 June. It is most likely that, in the hours after Tyler's death, Richard hurriedly countermanded the charters that he conceded that same morning and on the previous day. The new charter placed the Abbey and its buildings under his protection, and threatened grave punishment against any who inflicted any damage. Whereas the charter to Grindecobbe and Wallingford had only been endorsed by the King's own signet ring, the countermanding order had the force of the Great Seal of England, which implies that the King was now surrounded by the Chancellor and the apparatus of the government. This was a graphic illustration of the rapid change in the King's personal circumstances – from virtual hostage of the rebels to triumphant victor and hero of the hour.

The rebels clearly felt that they were running out of time, and they renewed pressure on Abbot de la Mare. At some point on 16 June de La Mare buckled and drew up a charter recognising St Albans as a borough and the townsmen as burgesses. This was followed on 17 June by the Abbot's own confirmation of the general manumission granted by Richard II to the men of Hertfordshire, three days earlier. In the Abbot's own charter to the men of St Albans, the boundaries of the Abbey and borough were defined, and, in a major concession, the Abbot relinquished the right of his bailiff to hold court within the franchise of the borough. Mindful of the ease with which their successes had been reversed in 1330, the townsmen then extorted from the Abbey a bond of £1,000 to keep good faith with the agreement, and a quitclaim of all rights he had previously claimed from the townsmen.

To the horror of Thomas Walsingham, the boundaries reverted to those that had been conceded by Abbot Hugh Eversdone in 1326, and the townsmen performed a ceremonial perambulation to celebrate their victory. This was no solemn pacing of the bounds, and had more of the character of a May Day or midsummer feast. 'With great clamour and tumult' the townsmen were accompanied by carts filled with bread and ale, and at certain symbolic boundary points they halted, and toasted their success. Walsingham stated explicitly that the choice of halting points was chosen to celebrate their success, which would seem to indicate that these had been long disputed between the town and the Abbey.[22] The walking of the bounds, which was a near repeat of that of 1326, formed part of a ritualised assertion of common custom, and it would play a part in the lives of English communities for many centuries to come.[23]

By 17 June news of the successes of the St Albans men had spread throughout Hertfordshire. Soon, the tenants of the Abbey's outlying estates at Barnet, Rickmansworth, Redburn and Watford were pressing for their own charters, which were granted to them on 17 and 18 June. As well as the general demands for manumission, each community also threw in its own special grievance – the men of Tring gained exemption tolls, while those of Barnet sought to erase the history of their villeinage by burning the Abbey's book of manor court rolls. There was also widespread demolition of enclosures, hedges and other obstructions to the common land that had been erected by the Abbey.

The men of Redburn levelled an entire embankment constructed to protect the Abbey's meadow at Pondsmead. Walsingham records that, within a matter of days, the St Albans townsmen had gained the active support of thirty-two other communities in the locality. Between 16 and 20 June, twenty charters of manumission were issued to communities under the Abbey's lordship. The fact that the last batch of charters – to Horwood, Shipton, Aston Abbots, Westwick and Newenham – was granted five days after Tyler's death, shows the extent to which even a county close to London had its own distinct chronology of insurrection.

The reasons for Abbot de la Mare's sudden and complete capitulation are not difficult to explain. Although he had received communication by 17 June that Sir Hugh Seagrave, the King's steward, and Sir Thomas Percy, were coming to his assistance, this did not materialise until 28 June. The King's own efforts had been concentrated in Essex in the days after the London revolt, and St Albans had remained a low priority for the royal council and the justices. Finally, a local knight, Sir Walter atte Lee, persuaded the royal council to entrust himself, Geoffrey Stukeley and Edward Benstead with a commission to restore peace between the Abbot and the men of the town.[24]

As rumours of this impending commission reached St Albans, the resolve of the townsmen began to crumble. But it is precisely at this time of pressure that Grindecobbe showed his mettle. Faced with the dispersal of many of his men, he urged them to be of good heart, reminding them that they enjoyed the support of eight of the nearest villages. On the morning of 29 June, a force of fifty men-at-arms and a large body of archers under Sir Walter atte Lee, arrived at St Albans, and were escorted into the town by Grindecobbe and his men. Invoking the powers that had been committed to him by the King, atte Lee summoned all of the townsmen to Deerfold Wood for nine o'clock that morning. The purpose of atte Lee's commission became clear when he ordered the townsmen to empanel a jury to testify about any crimes committed against the Abbey.[25] Unsurprisingly, the townsmen refused to do this, and also declined to surrender the charters that they had been granted. Stalemate ensued in the following days, but the writing was already on the wall for the St Albans insurgents. Effectively, the arrival of atte Lee on the morning of 29 June marked the end of the St Albans rising, and also the beginning of a depressing period of indictments, trials and executions.

But, for all its eventual failure, the St Albans rising demonstrated the remarkable determination and organisational skills of a group of ordinary men and women. Drawing on a common heritage of resistance to the Abbey's lordship, the townsmen were united by the clear aims of securing their status as burgesses, and refining their boundaries and communal privileges. But these hard and fast political and commercial aims were also expressed through a rich symbolic vocabulary. The removal of the mill-stones, the fixing of the rabbit to the pillory and the ceremonial feasting at the borough's boundaries were a powerful 'customary' response to the feudal lordship of the Abbey. Indeed, the burning of the old charters, and the extortion of confirmations of liberty from the Abbey, were little less than an attempt to rewrite and redefine the history and status of the community of St Albans. But, the arrival of Walter atte Lee and his men revealed how isolated and marginalised the men of St Albans had become. For all of their success in mobilising other communities – especially those under the Abbey's lordship – the townsmen had placed their faith in Wat Tyler and his men. There is an undeniable pathos to their expectations for deliverance by the London rebels, long after Tyler had been killed and his followers dispersed.

THE FEAR OF REVOLT IN LEICESTER

Henry Knighton wrote his account of the Great Rising from Leicester Abbey, and so his record of events there is extremely valuable, especially as (unlike Walsingham in St Albans) he did not appear to have a personal axe to grind. Throughout much of the east of England, the Great Rising was running on a different time-scale to that in London – a peculiarity which may have been partially due to the slowness of communications and lack of central co-ordination among the rebel groups. Significantly, the first news of the Great Rising was brought to Leicester by a messenger, warning the town that a large band of rebels was already approaching Market Harborough, a few miles away in Leicestershire.

One of the unusual factors about the threat to Leicester was that it had the result of uniting the townsmen against the external threat represented by the rebels. Unsure of how to proceed – and perhaps also concerned to bind the townspeople to whatever course of action was adopted – the mayor took advice about whether to resist the rebels (with the attendant risks of a violent sacking) or to admit them, and risk the wrath of their lord upon his return. The resolution was to resist the rebels, with the result that the town was thrown into a defensible state, and on the following morning 1,200 of the townsmen gathered on Gartree Hill, just outside the town walls, to await whatever came. The scratch militia waited in vain, as the messengers that they sent out came back without any news of the rebels' advance.

These rebels had set out from London some days before, and they had made no secret of their aim – to do to John of Gaunt's castle of Leicester what they had already done to the Savoy. As we have seen, the lord of Leicester was far away on the Scottish border, and the vulnerability of his property had become very clear during the London rising. On Sunday 16 or Monday 17 June Gaunt's wardrobe-keeper, William Oke, arrived in Leicester, with the intention of removing the Duke's possessions from the castle, and shifting them to a safer location.[26] Gaunt's possessions were duly put into carts and transported to Leicester Abbey, where Oke doubtless hoped that Abbot Kereby would keep them safe. But Abbot Kereby feared that if the rebels knew that he had taken in cartloads of Gaunt's possessions, then it might give them cause to sack his own house. Thus, the cartloads of wall hangings, tapestries and plate were taken back to the castle, where they were left exposed to the elements in the churchyard of St Mary de Castro.

The episode at Leicester illustrates the significant role played by rumour in the Great Rising. Henry Knighton notes that news reached Gaunt that his castle and possessions in Leicester had been destroyed – whereas nothing of the sort had happened.[27] Thus the men of Leicester waited, and the Duke's possessions remained in the carts, but the anticipated storm passed the town by. Although Leicester was spared an actual invasion, the experience of the Great Rising was no less real to the mayor, townsmen and monks.[28] Had the burghers taken a secret delight in arming themselves and awaiting the rebel band on Gartree Hill?

The Rising in Suffolk and Cambridgeshire

The revolt that broke out in Suffolk was one of the longest lasting county disturbances in the summer of 1381, and its genesis can be traced to the actions of the Essex rebels before their march on London. The dominant personality in the Suffolk revolt was one John Wrawe, a former priest from the locality of Sudbury. However, beyond this bare fact, little more is known about the man who mobilised the men of Suffolk.[29] On Wednesday 12 June Wrawe led a band of Essex men to Liston-on-Stour, on the border with Suffolk, and there he proclaimed that he had come to redress the grievances of all men. Walsingham believed that Wrawe had already been in contact with Wat Tyler in London. But, given that Tyler was still on the road to London on the evening of Wednesday 12 June, it seems unlikely that he had made contact with Wrawe at this time. Wrawe then directed his men to Long Melford, and emissaries were also sent to Sudbury. Their first target was the manor of Overhall, one of the many properties of Sir Richard Lyons, the hated financier who would perish in London two days later. After the attack on Overhall, Wrawe's men marched on Cavendish, which they reached on Thursday 13 June. It would seem that they had been drawn to Cavendish because of news that Chief Justice Cavendish had stored his goods in the parish church. Through the sympathy of Ralph Somerton, a Sudbury dyer, a key was found and when the church tower was unlocked various items of plate and clothing were recovered. Having raised a good thirst, Wrawe's men repaired to 'Onewene's Tavern' in Melford Green, where they celebrated their progress with a pipe of red wine.[30]

Wrawe and his men entered Bury St Edmunds on the morning of Friday 14 June, and crowded down Cooks Row towards the great gates of the abbey.[31] The next stage on Wrawe's itinerary was Bury St Edmunds, which was reached late in the evening of Thursday 13 June. As in St Albans, there was a legacy of conflict between the town and Abbey. But in Bury this was further compli-cated by a prolonged vacancy in the abbacy, arising from a disputed election. Following the death of Abbot John Brinkley in December 1378, the monks had elected one of their own number, John Tymworth, as his successor. However, Edmund Brounfield, one of the representatives of the Benedictine Order in the papal court, and himself a monk of Bury with considerable influence and property in the town, had already used his access to the Pope to secure his own provision to the abbacy. The dispute had come to a head when Brounfield returned to England with his papal letters of appoint-ment. In the interim, governance of the Abbey had devolved to the Prior, John Cambridge, who had strongly opposed Brounfield's candidacy. When Brounfield eventually reached Bury, his friends in the town had him invested with the staff and mitre of the Abbot, notwithstanding the opposition of Prior Cambridge, and the fact that he had received the votes of only seventeen of the fifty-nine monks – who decisively favoured Tymworth. But Brounfield's success was short-lived, as provision to an English benefice by the papacy had been a statutory offence since 1351.[32] The unfortunate Brounfield found himself under arrest soon after his return, and by the time of the outbreak of revolt, he was incarcerated in Nottingham Castle.[33]

Although the Bury men were not in a position to lever Brounfield into the abbacy, the revolt gave them the opportunity to vent their hatred of Prior Cambridge. As in the case of the St Albans men, the townsmen of Bury looked for external support in the prosecution of their campaign, and they sent for John Wrawe and his men. They arrived on the evening of 13 June, and set about attacking the monastic buildings. Like the Prior of St Albans, John Cambridge had already made his getaway from Bury, but whereas the former had escaped to the safety of Northumberland, the latter had hoped merely to reach Ely, where he hoped that he might be harboured. Cambridge had found himself a guide, who had escorted him to the outskirts of Newmarket, but, fearing to enter the town, he remained concealed in a local wood. However, his guide then betrayed him and he was returned to John Wrawe at Mildenhall, where he was beheaded on the morning of Saturday 15 June. Like those of the men beheaded at the Tower, the head of John Cambridge was fixed on a pike, and was carried back to Bury.[34]

During the pursuit of Prior Cambridge, another group had been sent out to Thetford. Once again, the composition of the Suffolk rebel group was a fairly broad cross-section, as the group sent to Thetford included Geoffrey Parfray, vicar of All Saints' Church, Sudbury, and an esquire, Thomas Montchensey. They appear to have threatened the town with the punishment of John Wrawe and, on the strength of this, extracted a payment of forty marks of gold. Another case of criminal extortion was perpetrated by one of the gentlemen adherents of John Wrawe – Sir Thomas Cornerd. He broke into the house of John Rokwood, and extorted from him five marks, which he then delivered to Wrawe. The fact that Cornerd was only allowed to keep 40s of this sum suggests that Wrawe was able to command a degree of obedience from among his followers, even those who were undoubtedly his social superiors.

The prime target of the Suffolk rebels was Sir John Cavendish, a Chief Justice of the King's Bench, now chancellor of the University of Cambridge, and a substantial landowner in East Anglia.[35] Cavendish's principal residence was in Bury, and, like John Cambridge, he had already fled in advance of the arrival of Wrawe's men. However Cavendish, like Cambridge, was too well known in East Anglia to effect an escape, and the rebels overtook him at Lakenheath. During the subsequent trial of two of the men indicted for Cavendish's murder, John Poter of Somerton and John Pedder of Fordham, the Chief Justice's chamberlain, John Pole, testified that he had been heading for the ferry over the Brandon, and that he would have escaped, but for the actions of a woman, called Katherine Gamen, who pushed the waiting boat into the river (it is worth noting that the escape of Archbishop Sudbury from the Tower was also foiled by a woman – although her name is not known). Cavendish was apprehended on the river bank by one John Pedder of Fordham, and beheaded at the hands of Matthew Miller.[36]

The ghoulish sense of humour of the Suffolk rebels was indulged when Cavendish's head was returned to Bury. He and Prior John Cambridge had been close associates, a friendship celebrated by the rebels who made the head of Cavendish confess into the ear of Cambridge, and then the two exchanged kisses. The heads of Cavendish and Cambridge were joined on the pillory at Bury by that of John Lakenheath, a monk who had been responsible for managing the Abbey's lordship over the town and its outling tenants.[37] In some respects, the rising in Bury mirrored that of St Albans, as the townsmen took advantage of the disturbed state of the county to confiscate the Abbey's documents, and extort the concession of a charter of liberties. Whereas the townsmen of St Albans had looked to a supposed charter of Offa, those of Bury looked to that of Cnut, who had founded the Abbey in 1020. This political obsession for the charters of pre-Conquest kings may have some echoes of a lingering English resentment against an 'alien' political and social elite, and the preservation of a popular memory (albeit seriously misconceived) of a Saxon state of common liberty. Echoes of this political discourse would recur in the English Civil War, when the myth of 'The Norman Yoke' enjoyed considerable currency among the radical Protestant sects.

In the short-term, Wrawe proved to be even more successful than Grindecobbe in gaining the support of hamlets and villages in the locality of Bury St Edmunds. However, the pattern and intensity of the violence in Suffolk differed from that in Hertfordshire. Whereas the St Albans men had resorted to violence only as a last resort, and had placed their faith in the concession of charters, the Suffolk rebels indulged in much more private score-settling. Oman was quick to dismiss the titles supposedly conferred on Wrawe and his ally Robert Westbrom, 'Kings of the Commons', as either a ridiculous conceit or an invention of the pen of Thomas Walsingham.[38] However, to dismiss the significance of ritualised identities may be to ignore a strong sense of county particularism among the rebels – that may well have been stimulated in response to the intrusive tax-raising and judicial commissions that had been issuing from Westminster during the previous few years.

The revolt in Ipswich appears to have been distinct from that which had broken out in the vicinity of Bury. Around Friday 14 June, groups of insurgents were gathering south of Ipswich, and, two days later, entered the town. Their leaders appear to have been two local men – John Battisford, like Wrawe a parson, and Thomas Sampson, a tenant farmer. The rebels were admitted to Ipswich without any resistance, and, as in the case of the other towns, their violence was carefully targeted. The houses of the Archdeacon of Suffolk and of John Cobat, a collector of the Poll Tax, were attacked and looted. The property of the Suffolk archdeaconry was singled out because the office was in the hands of a non-resident foreign cardinal.

However, in the hunt for their main target, a justice of the peace, Edmund Lakenheath, the rebels were thwarted. Although they succeeded in ransacking his house at Gislingham and stealing cattle from his nearby estates, Lakenheath himself reached the coast and escaped by boat. But the price of Lakenheath's escape would be very high, as he fell into the hands of the admiral of France, and ransomed himself at the price of 500 marks.[39] Another county official who suffered considerable losses was Roger Wolfreston, who had served as escheator of Suffolk. On Sunday 16 June his house at Culpho was despoiled and large numbers of cattle and horses stolen. One of the most prominent buildings to suffer attack was Mettingham Castle, the residence of Sir Roger de Boys, which was assaulted twice by men under John Wrawe. In addition to the looting of precious objects and furnishings, the men also removed and burned the court rolls – a pattern of destruction common to all of the county risings.[40] Indeed, the violence in Suffolk continued in this vein until the arrival of the Earl of Suffolk on 23 June at the head of 500 men-at-arms.

Although the Suffolk rising shared characteristics with the disturbances in the other affected counties, its extent, duration and the intensity of the violence marked it out. It had the contradictory characteristics of a strong element of 'class war' against unpopular landlords, but also numerous incidents of criminality perpetrated by propertied individuals against their enemies. The knights Roger Bacon and Thomas Cornerd were two of the highest ranking individuals to participate in any of the disturbances of 1381. Therefore, the hierarchical allegiances in Suffolk sustained serious damage in the period of revolt from 10 June to the end of that month. The administrative structure – represented by the sheriff, escheator and commissioners of the peace – was completely overwhelmed by the momentum of popular violence. In his detailed research into the social structure of Suffolk, Christopher Dyer has highlighted the tensions arising from the resistance of landlords to the demands of their increasingly prosperous tenants who were anxious to escape their villein status. It comes as no surprise that the Great Rising was felt most forcefully in the wealthiest counties, where seigniorial intransigence chafed harshly against the ambitions of the commons.[41]

Just as revolt had spread across the Suffolk boundary from Essex, so it reached Cambridgeshire on 15 June. Part of the Cambridgeshire rising appears to have been a contiguous infection from Suffolk, and the eastern parts of the county came under the influence of John Wrawe's men. Other rebels were motivated by John Greyston, a Bottisham man who had witnessed the events in London, and rushed back to Cambridgeshire before Tyler's death. A third group operating around Cambridge appeared to be more 'indigenous' to the county, and was led by two gentlemen, John Hanchach and Geoffrey Cobbe.[42] As Oman notes, the patterns of violence in Cambridgeshire were broadly similar to those in the other affected counties – with the houses of governmental officers and unpopular landowners, both lay and ecclesiastical, succumbing to the flames. Perhaps the delayed arrival of the revolt in Cambridgeshire had given the elite of the county the slim margin of time necessary to make good their escape. But the unfortunate Edmund Walsingham, a justice of the peace, fell into the hands of the men of Ely, who beheaded him on Monday 17 June.

The distinctive feature of the Cambridgeshire rising was the attitude of the rebels to the University of Cambridge. As in St Albans and Bury, Cambridge had a legacy of conflict between the townsmen and the ecclesiastical corporations. On 1 May 1381 the townsmen had coerced Chancellor Cavendish into surrendering the deeds of the University's privileges, and tension within Cambridge had been growing throughout the Spring. This was not just anti-ecclesiastical resentment by the poorer inhabitants of Cambridge, but a general hatred of the University that united all, including the mayor, Edmund Redmeadow, who would play a leading part in the events of June 1381.

It is likely that it was the activities of the gentleman rebel, John Hanchach, in nearby Shudy Camps that ignited the Cambridge rising on 15 June 1381. Meeting at the front of the Guildhall, the rebels nominated two of their number, James and Thomas Grantchester, as their captains. But there were also powerful forces behind this popular movement, including Mayor Redmeadow and others within the town's governing elite. From the outset, the rebels directed their ire against the leadership of the University.

As the chancellor, John Cavendish, had already been slain, their energies were dedicated to the capture of the University Bedel, William Wigmore. Wisely, Wigmore had already fled Cambridge, but his property, like that of Cavendish, felt the full wrath of the townsmen.

Although Cavendish and Wigmore had come to symbolise the hated University hierarchy, the townsmen were no less hostile towards the scholars and masters. The institution that was singled out for their hostile intentions was Corpus Christi College. Although by no means the wealthiest or largest college in the University, Corpus Christi was obnoxious to the townsmen for several reasons. Since its foundation in 1352 by the Guild of Corpus Christi, the college had acquired a large number of properties in the town through bequests. These were now rented from Corpus Christi as 'candle rents' – the proceeds going to maintain the functioning of the College. Therefore, by the 1380s, Corpus Christi had become a substantial proprietor within the town of Cambridge, with as many as one-sixth of the town's tenants owing it some form of rent. It also could claim a connection which had become an even greater liability by 1381. Its most munificent early patron and benefactor had been Henry of Grosmont, Duke of Lancaster, and it continued to enjoy the favour of his son-in-law and heir, John of Gaunt.[43] On 21 January 1381 Gaunt had successfully lobbied his royal nephew to grant Corpus Christi a charter licensing it to acquire additional lands and rents.

On the night of 15 June the College was stormed and subjected to a thorough ransacking. Not satisfied with an impressive haul of books, plate, muniments and furnishings, the townsmen set about the fixtures – sparing neither doors nor windows. The damage was so great that in 1384 the crown paid it £80 towards the recovery of its losses, and permitted it to sell its remaining houses in Cambridge to raise further capital.[44] Other buildings to suffer damage included St Mary's Church, which was not only despoiled of its plate, but also of the University archives that were stored there. The University library, which was stored in chests in the house of the Carmelites, also caught the attention of the rebels, and its books, together with the archives and charters, fed a great bonfire that had been built on Market Square. As with the burning of the Savoy, political destruction appears to have predominated over the desire for criminal gain. Legend has it that a local woman, Margery Starre cried 'Away with the learning of the clerks, away with it!' as the University's treasures were consumed by the flames.[45]

As in St Albans and Bury, the Cambridge townsmen were attempting to redefine their relationship to an ecclesiastical corporation that dominated their community. In a charter drawn up by the townsmen on 16 June, the University surrendered all of its royal privileges, and promised that in future it would only enter pleas in the court of the borough. To ensure compliance the town forced the University to make over a bond for £3,000. Having achieved their aims against the University, the townsmen then turned their attentions against the priory of Barnwell, which lay a little distance outside the town. The origins of popular resentment against Barnwell lay in a dispute over its supposed enclosure and blocking of a long established common pasturage known as The Drove. Like the rebels in other towns and villages, the Cambridge men took matters into their own hands and demolished the priory's fences.

The Cambridge revolt was a brief affair, collapsing upon the arrival of Bishop Despenser of Norwich, with an armed retinue at his back, on 18/19 June. But the Cambridge rising did reveal the capacity for anti-clerical resentment to act as a powerful adhesive, uniting the richest burgesses with the poorest commoners. For the townsmen, the University was not a seat of learning, but a parasite that exploited its privileges at their expense, and to the disparagement of their own liberties.

Throughout this period Ely had also witnessed serious disturbances. Bands set out from Ely to wreck the houses of county officers, and other familiar targets. Some spread the rising into Huntingdonshire, but there appeared to be no 'indigenous' rising in the county. Indeed, the band of men from Ely who attempted to sack the estates of Ramsey Abbey were unable to attract any local support, and so returned to Cambridgeshire having failed in their mission.[46]

THE RISING IN NORFOLK

On the same day that Wrawe and his men were entering Bury (14 June), Norfolk was experiencing its first disturbances. Herbert Eiden's research has shown that while there were indigenous rebel bands in Norfolk, the conflagration was fed by the deliberate spreading of revolt from neighbouring Suffolk. Geoffrey Parfray, Wrawe's accomplice, crossed The Great Ouse and entered Thetford, at the head of a band of about sixty men, and extorted twenty marks of gold from the town. It seems that their numbers were soon strengthened by Norfolk men, who pushed northwards into the centre of the county, operating in small groups. That one of these groups was led by Thomas, son of Sir Thomas Gissing, a prominent local man, confirms that this was not a general protest against landed proprietors, but was a revolt with strong political motivations.[47] As in Kent, Essex and London, the rebels were highly discriminating in their choice of targets. Eiden notes that John of Gaunt and Bury St Edmunds Abbey lost estate records through arson at Methwold, Hilgay and Southery. It appears that men from Cambridgeshire crossed into Norfolk to join the attack on the house of Nicholas Massingham, JP, at Hilgay. Indeed, as elsewhere in the revolt, justices of the peace were particularly singled-out for attack. Edmund Gournay (who also happened to be the steward of Gaunt's estates in the county) and his fellow justice, John Holkham, fled by boat westwards along the Norfolk coastline, and were pursued as far as Burnham.[48]

Whereas the rebels in southern and western Norfolk had been in contact with men from Suffolk and Cambridgeshire, those operating north of Norwich began their revolt without any external support. Their rising appeared to have originated in the north-east of the county, in North Walsham, Scottow and Felmingham.[49] This band was led by Geoffrey Litster, a dyer from Felmingham, but it also gained the services of another high-status rebel, Sir Roger Bacon of Baconsthorpe. Setting aside Sir John Newton (who appears to have been more of a hostage cum-go-between for the Kentish rebels), Sir Roger Bacon appears to have been the highest ranking participant in the 1381 rising, and yet his exact motivations remain puzzling. He may well have shared in the broader popular hostility to the governmental, diplomatic and military failings of the age, while also harbouring some local grievance against one of the local magnates or justices. But if he did harbour such a grievance, none has so far been discovered.

Litster communicated with other potential rebels through two men, John Gentilhomme and Richard Filmond, whom he sent as messengers to agitate for support in the villages of north Norfolk. This campaign must have met with some success, as Litster and his companions felt sufficiently confident to move on Norwich between 16-17 June.[50] This was indeed an ambitious target – more significant than Cambridge or Bury St Edmunds – as it was both the seat of a bishop, and also one of the main manufacturing and trading cities in the kingdom. Just as the Kentish rebels had summoned men to join them on Blackheath before entering London, those of Norfolk gathered on Mousehold Heath before their march on Norwich (in 1549 Mousehold Heath would become the focus of another Norfolk rising, that led by Robert Kett).[51]

Faced with a growing force of rebels just outside the city, the men of Norwich opened their gates to Litster and his men. The occasion of the rebels' entry to Norwich gave Froissart the opportunity to put a dramatic gloss on the story. He claims that the defence of the city had been entrusted to Sir Robert Salle, a man of humble birth who owed his rank entirely to his courage and skill on the battlefield. According to Froissart, Litster sought to parley with Salle outside the city gates, with the intention of inducing his defection to the rebel cause. Insulted by the suggestion that he should place his low birth before his knightly honour, Salle trusted to his sword and he met his death among an improbably large pile of his dismembered assailants. In fact, Salle's murder at Norwich is likely to have been far less glamorous, and, according to Thomas Walsingham, he was beaten to death by one of his own villeins.[52] Once admitted to Norwich, the rebels followed the predictable pattern of attacking individuals and buildings associated with government and the law. An unfortunate JP, Reginald Eccles, was captured and butchered with knives at the town's pillory.[53]

Given that the outbreak of revolt in Norfolk lagged behind that of the south-eastern counties by almost a week, the lack of preparedness on the part of the local lords seems almost negligent. William Ufford, earl of Suffolk, who had been residing at one of his Norfolk manors, was so shocked by the news of the rising that (according to Walsingham he fled the county by a circuitous route to Hertfordshire, and then made his way to the king, disguised as a valet of Sir Roger Boys. Although hardly a chivalrous response for a Knight of The Garter, Ufford had at least avoided falling into the hands of the rebels – and in that respect was more successful than a number of his fellow Norfolk landowners, including Lord Scales, Sir William Morley, Sir John Brewes, Sir Stephen Hales and the unfortunate Sir Robert Salle. According to Walsingham, Litster styled himself 'king of the Commons' and appointed Stephen Hales as his carver, while Morley and Brewes were sent to London in order to gain the king's pardon for the Norfolk rebels. If Walsingham is to be believed, Litster's adoption of this regal title was not entirely make-believe, as he supposedly presided over his own court at Thorpe Market, and banqueted in the hall of Norwich Castle. Litster's regal gysing and carnivalesque behaviour

may conceal a more important message about the local particularism voiced by many of the rebels. The Norfolk men, like those of
Kent and Essex, had a strong sense of county identity, and may well
have regarded the growing influence of the royal court and the
legal establishment as a threat to this.[54]

Unique among the county risings, that of Norfolk was not
extinguished by a royal commission of justices backed by soldiers,
but collapsed through the agency of a local magnate, Henry
Despenser, bishop of Norwich. Like John of Gaunt, Despenser had
avoided capture by the rebels through pure chance, as he had been
staying at his Rutland manor of Burley, just outside Oakham.
According to Walsingham, he was attended by only eight men-at-
arms and a handful of archers, but, undeterred by the size of the
rebel force, set out on the road south to Norfolk. At Icklingham he
met Sir William Morley and Sir John Brewes, en route to London
to deliver Litster's message to the king. At first it would seem that
the two knights were afraid to tell Despenser that they were prisoners of the rebels, but they eventually took courage and
denounced their escorts, who were promptly beheaded. To adver-
tise his intentions more clearly, Despenser had two severed heads
displayed at Newmarket.

News of Despenser's advance into Norfolk appears to have
mobilised both the rebels and loyalists. Walsingham states that the
local gentry were inspired (or shamed) at the sight of Despenser in
armour at the head of his retinue, and resolved to join him. It seems
that, on entering Norfolk, Despenser's men had wheeled eastwards,
as the rebels attacked The Abbey of St Benet's Holme on the night
of 23-4 June in the belief that they were resting there. Eiden notes
that the rebels were still in sufficient heart to protest against
Despenser in the villages north of the river Bure.[55] Eventually, on
25/6 June, Despenser's retinue and the men of Geoffrey Litster
engaged at North Walsham, near to where the north Norfolk rising
had begun. That the two forces should meet at North Walsham begs
a number of questions. Had Litster abandoned Norwich for the

more familiar territory of north Norfolk, or had he been shadowing Despenser's force, perhaps in the hope that more local men would join him in an attack on the bishop's retinue? Ultimately, Litster's strategy cannot be known. Moreover, what actually happened at North Walsham has been subject to disputed interpretations.

In Walsingham's colourful and near-contemporary account, the rebels had blocked the road through North Walsham by excavating a ditch, and erected barricades from doors, gates and fences. In this version, Despenser was determined to give battle and rode into the middle of the rebel defences with a couched lance 'like a wild boar gnashing its teeth, sparing neither himself nor his enemies'. Vicious hand-to-hand fighting followed, with Despenser in the midst of the action. Those rebels who had survived the initial onslaught attempted to flee on carts that had been drawn up behind their lines, but were cut down as they attempted to make good their escape. Soon after, Litster was captured and brought into Despenser's presence. Pronouncing the sentence of drawing, hanging and beheading on Litster, Despenser then heard his confession, and allowed him the small mercy of supporting his head, 'lest it bounce on the ground', while he was dragged off to be hanged.[56]

But a corrective to this dramatic account was offered by John Capgrave, who, although writing in the following century, had been born at Lynn in 1393, and so may have had personal contact with individuals who had witnessed the events at North Walsham. Capgrave claimed that Despenser had first come to Thorpe Market, some miles to the north-west of North Walsham, where he had proclaimed that all who wished well to the kingdom should join him. But when Despenser reached North Walsham the rebels were so intimidated by his retinue that they dispersed without resistance, and that Litster was captured while taking flight in a nearby wheat field.[57] This corrective was long accepted until Eiden noted that the contemporary manor court rolls for North Walsham record the violent deaths of a number of local men in June 1381 at the hands of gentlemen.[58] Therefore, although

Walsingham's account may not be free of embellishment, it seems likely that Litster's men put up more than token resistance at North Walsham, while the violent end of 'the king of the Commons of Norfolk' is not in doubt.

Unsurprisingly, the death of Litster and his accomplices at Walsham had the desired effect, and the rising in Norfolk collapsed in the face of Despenser's growing company of knights and gentlemen. The rising in Cambridge was suppressed by the arrival of Despenser's men, who despatched some of the leading rebels who fell into their hands. In spite of their leading roles in the East Anglian rising, both Sir Roger Bacon and Thomas Gissing escaped the gallows, and were eventually pardoned after a period of imprisonment.

The risings that occurred in the southern and eastern counties during and after the rebel invasion of London should not be regarded as peripheral to the story of 1381. In terms of participants, the East Anglian risings may well have rivalled the invasion of London, and some men are likely to have been in arms in Norfolk and Suffolk for almost two weeks before the full weight of the royal suppression was felt. Indeed, there is a strong case that the centre of balance of the revolt be shifted to the east of London, given that the revolt had its genesis in East Kent and Essex, and that the fiercest rebel resistance was encountered in East Anglia. But for all of the predictable burnings, sackings and lynchings, the risings in the counties also revealed the political maturity and sophistication of some of the rebel communities. The men of St Albans stand out for their command of a richly symbolic political vocabulary, and their efforts to redefine their relationship to the Abbey through the generally peaceful means of charters and the walking of boundaries.

However, the county risings also highlight the apparent catatonia – either through fear or surprise – of the political and landed elites in the counties affected by revolt. Bishop Despenser stands out all the more because he was alone in attempting to mobilise the established political hierarchy without any assistance from the King and the royal council. In spite of the efforts of Despenser, the social order of much of southern and eastern England was left in tatters. The challenge now facing the crown was not merely to punish those who had risen, but to do so in a way that created the unmistakable impression of a restored social order.

7

THE AFTERMATH

The Restoration of Royal Control

The seven days from Monday 10 June 1381 stand out in English history because of the evaporation of royal and noble authority in the southern and eastern counties. Even during the worst periods of civil war in 1140–1, 1216–17 and 1322, the bonds of social hierarchy had remained substantially intact.[1] But even after Tyler's death on 15 June, the crown's ability to project its authority was hindered by the escalating violence in East Anglia. What was the overall impact of this violence on the governance of the kingdom in the spring and summer of 1381? In addition to the deaths of the Chancellor, Treasurer and Chief Justice, a number of local officers had also been murdered. But, as Ormrod has suggested, the burning and looting of records may have had a greater short-term impact than the loss of personnel. Prominent victims of record burning included the Chancery and Exchequer, The Temple, Lambeth Palace and The Duchy of Lancaster, as well as several private bureaucracies, including those of the Countess of Hereford and Essex, the Bishop of Norwich and The University of Cambridge. In the case of the royal records it seems that the impact of the revolt was fairly ephemeral, as much of what was lost appears to have been in the nature of 'working drafts' rather than continuous runs of records over many years. This has led Ormrod to suggest that the courts and the exchequer may have ceased operating during The Rising in order to minimise the vulnerability of personnel and paperwork alike.[2]

What remains perplexing is the general absence of individual or collective acts of resistance by the nobility. The personal initiatives of Bishop Despenser in Norfolk and Sir Walter atte Lee in Hertfordshire stand out precisely because they were so exceptional.[3] Was this cowardice on the part of the nobility? Some of the lords and knights of East Anglia and the south-eastern counties were undoubtedly paralysed by the speed and early successes of the rebels. However, many of the most experienced knights and men-at-arms were still serving in the expedition of the King's uncle, Edmund, Earl of Cambridge. (Richard would face a similar problem in 1399, when he returned from Ireland to resist his cousin's usurpation, but without the bulk of his army.) In 1381 the northern lords were too far from London to make any difference to the early days of the suppression, and their principal responsibility lay in the defence of the Scottish marches.

As soon as the King and council had regained control of London, efforts were made to stamp royal authority on the suppression of the Great Rising. On 15 June Sir Robert Knolles, Sir Nicholas Brembre and Sir Robert Launde (all of whom had proven their loyalty at Smithfield) were ordered to restore order in the city of London. Five days later Thomas, Earl of Buckingham, the King's youngest uncle, and Sir Robert Tresilian, the Chief Justice, received a sweeping commission to enforce the King's peace throughout the kingdom. A special commission was also appointed to Kent, to be led by Robert Ashton, constable of Dover, John Clinton, Sir Thomas Trivet and Stephen Valence.

Similar orders were issued to the mayors and sheriffs to restore order in their localities.[4] But the most important expression of the crown's recovery was its issuing of orders from 30 June commanding villeins to submit to those same conditions that they had fought so hard to throw off during the Rising. On 2 July all of the charters of manumission that had been granted by the crown were formally rescinded and cancelled.[5] Later the crown issued specific instructions to the villeins of the Earl of Arundel, the Countess of Norfolk, and of the priories of Wymondham, Barnwell and Dartford, commanding them to perform their accustomed services.[6] Some of these estates, especially those of the Countess of Norfolk and the Prioress of Dartford, were in areas heavily affected by insurrection, and had sustained substantial losses.

The first major punitive action taken by the crown was on 17 June (while the East Anglian revolt was still gaining momentum), when an expedition of twelve horsemen and twenty-five archers set out from London for Kent under the leadership of the King's elder half-brother, Thomas Holand, Earl of Kent, and Sir Thomas Trivet. On 4 June they began to hear indictments at Maidstone, before moving to Rochester.[7] From about 20 June commissions were also sent in the eastern counties. The Earl of Suffolk, with 500 men-at-arms at his back (a fair contrast to his previous guise of a knight's valet) was sent into Suffolk. From 27 June his commission heard the testimonies of juries at Mildenhall, Hadleigh, Sudbury and Clare. On 6 July he moved his inquiry into Norfolk, and heard further indictments at Norwich, Hacking and Yarmouth. At the same time, Hugh, Lord la Zouche was leading a similar commission in Cambridgeshire.[8]

The commissions in Essex were entrusted to Sir Thomas Percy and to the King's youngest uncle, Buckingham, who held great estates in the county through his wife Eleanor Bohun. The first Essex sessions opened on 25 June at Chelmsford, in the centre of Buckingham's estates.[9] His fellow justices were drawn from his own neighbours and leading members of his affinity – Lord

Fitzwalter, Sir Thomas Mandeville and Sir John Harleston.[10] Such a large force of men and their retainers was necessary because of the continuing violence in the county.

Those Essex men who were still in arms resolved to resist Buckingham's commission, and made their stand at Billericay. Adopting the defensive tactics used by the Norfolk rebels at North Walsham, the Essex men constructed barricades and ditches, reinforced with stakes – presumably to deter cavalry. On 28 June Buckingham's men attacked, and the predictable result was a massacre, although whether 500 men perished, as Walsingham claims, is doubtful.[11]

While the commission under Buckingham was operating at Chelmsford, Sir Robert Tresilian and William Morrers had commenced hearings at Havering on 26 June. After hearing a number of indictments, Tresilian's commission relocated to Chelmsford to take over from that of Buckingham, which had moved to Colchester.[12] At Chelmsford Tresilian heard detailed depositions relating to the very beginnings of the Rising, as jurors related how Thomas Baker of Fobbing, with John Geoffrey, and more than eighty of their neighbours, spread revolt among the local hamlets and villages.[13] Prescott concluded that Tresilian's Essex commission inflicted thirty-one capital sentences – of these twelve were subjected to the additional penalty of being dragged to the gallows.[14] Richard II himself took an active interest in the Essex hearings, and set out from London for Chelmsford on 1 July, where he remained for seven days, before proceeding to the royal manor of Havering.[15] Once he had completed his hearings in Essex, Tresilian moved on to St Albans on 13 July and presided over the trial of John Ball, who had been captured in Coventry.

After the pacification of Essex, the Earl and Countess of Buckingham, escorted by 200 men-at-arms, rode the breadth of the kingdom to quell a disturbance in Gloucester. The route would have been well known to the Earl, as many of his wife's inherited estates lay in Monmouth.[16] On 5 July the Earl of Northumberland was commissioned to lead a force of men-at-arms into Yorkshire, and in particular, to quell the disturbances in Scarborough.[17] The appointments of Buckingham and Northumberland are an important reminder that, although concentrated in the south and east, the Great Rising was felt in the west and north as well.

The men indicted before the judicial commissions faced a broad range of charges. Some, including those leading rebels who had survived the early days of suppression, were convicted on the basis of their notoriety, while others faced very specific charges. One frequently levelled charge was that of waging war against the King, or aiding his enemies. These came close to the statutory definition of treason, but the juries stopped short of stating this explicitly, probably because of confusion as to the letter of the law. The Great Treason Statute of 1352 had been framed with high political misdemeanours in mind, and its applicability to the crimes of the Great Rising was never defined.[18] Many more were indicted and tried on vaguer charges, such as being 'a common burner of books' or a 'common raiser of men'. The swearing of oaths of confederacy to resist all lordship was another common charge. A number of unusual offences were detected during the trials of summer 1381, including the demolition of dwelling places through the use of hooks and ropes, or by the more brutal method of piling stones on the roof.[19]

In addition to the royal commissions, many private prosecutions were pursued through the Court of Common Pleas. In most cases these were brought by individuals seeking redress for losses sustained either to land, buildings or moveable goods. These pleas revealed the range of material losses sustained – everything from weapons and armour through to livestock, furniture and even cured meat. But private actions for trespass were of limited effectiveness as, for obvious reasons, the defendants were unlikely to answer the charges in person. Prescott has highlighted the case of Bishop Despenser, who accused fifty individuals of having burned his manorial records at Hevingham, but was unable to compel their attendance at court. John of Gaunt made great efforts to secure the indictment of those Londoners whom he held responsible for the destruction of the Savoy, but, like many other property owners, he enjoyed only limited success in this.[20] Herbert Eiden has highlighted the case of Henry Lomynour, a prosperous burgess of Norwich, who indicted 600 named individuals for the attack against his property there on 17 June 1381. But this list needs to be treated with the greatest of caution, as it is implausible that so many men would have focused their efforts on a single property, or that Lomynour had a team of scribes standing by to take down their details in the midst of the chaos. In fact, it seems most likely that victims of the rebels exchanged lists of their alleged attackers, resulting in a snowballing of composite indictments, perhaps in the hope that at least a few of the rebels would be punished, even for crimes committed in locations that they could not have visited'.[21]

In the Parliament of November 1381, a series of general pardons were issued to the rebels, and also to those lords and knights who had committed extra-judicial killings, and had inflicted other sentences without due process during the aftermath of the Rising. However, a number of named individuals were excluded from the general pardon, and proceedings continued against them for many months in the King's Bench and for several years in Common Pleas. Prescott concludes that nearly 300 private actions were brought – the last being as late as 1387.[22]

THE TRIALS OF THE REBEL LEADERS

The suppression of the revolt brought a large haul of prisoners into crown hands, including some of its most notorious leaders – among them Jack Straw, John Wrawe, John Ball, and William Grindecobbe. Their trials and executions marked a savage phase of vengeance, and sent a clear political message, perhaps intended to complement the words attributed to the King during his Essex tour: 'Rustics you were and rustics you are still; you will remain in bondage, not as before but incomparably harsher'.[23]

The first trial of a major leader was that of Jack Straw, who was apprehended in London shortly after the death of Tyler. In spite of the subsequent fame of Jack Straw, reliable details of his trial and execution are lacking, and it is difficult to credit as believable the lengthy gallows speech attributed to him by Walsingham. Even the day of Straw's execution is difficult to pinpoint, but it seems likely that his severed head joined that of Tyler on London Bridge.[24]

Unlike Geoffrey Litster, John Wrawe had managed to escape from East Anglia, but he did not remain at liberty for long, and was probably captured before the end of June 1381. On 10 July 1381 he was brought to trial before the sheriffs of London. After making confession, Wrawe turned approver against twenty-four of his named erstwhile accomplices, including the knight, Thomas Cornerd, the esquires, John Talmache and Thomas Montchensey, and Geoffrey Parfray, the vicar of All Saints, Sudbury. In spite of Wrawe's full confession, and his turning King's evidence, on 6 May 1382 he was condemned by Chief Justice Tresilian to be drawn and hanged.[25] Many of those whom he betrayed, including Cornerd and Talmache, were more fortunate and gained their liberty after a period of imprisonment.

The most detailed accounts of the proceedings against the rebel leaders came from the pen of Thomas Walsingham, who may well have witnessed the trials and executions of William Grindecobbe and of John Ball in St Albans. Following the arrival of Sir Walter atte Lee, there had been something of a stalemate in St Albans, as the townsmen refused to surrender the charters that they had extorted from the Abbey. Tension remained high in the town, but Abbot de la Mare felt sufficiently confident to seize Grindecobbe and have him removed to the gaol at Hertford, escorted by the Abbey's esquires. Once there, he was released on bail, and returned to St Albans. In spite of the serious charges now facing him, Grindecobbe renewed his call to the townsmen to resist the

Abbot. Soon after he was returned to Hertford gaol, to await trial before the royal justices. The prospect of the imminent arrival of the King himself frightened the townsmen into coming to a last minute agreement with the Abbey.[26]

On 13 July a fearsome array of knights, men-at-arms and archers arrived in St Albans, with the King and Chief Justice Tresilian at their head.[27] The Moot Hall was chosen as the location for the sessions of the King's Bench, which was doubtless intended to impress and intimidate the townsmen. Tresilian established an uncompromising tone with his first order – that the millstones extracted by the townsmen be restored to the Abbey's precincts. William Grindecobbe and three of his leading accomplices were delivered from the gaol at Hertford, and immediately remanded into custody in St Albans.[28]

But Grindecobbe would have to wait, as there was more important business for Tresilian. John Ball, whose preaching had done so much to inflame the rebels in Kent at the beginning of June, had been apprehended at Coventry. According to Walsingham, he was brought to trial before Tresilian in the Moot Hall on 14 July, and was confronted with the rhyming letters (discussed in chapter three) that he had supposedly written. Confessing to the charges brought against him, Ball was sentenced to be drawn, hanged and quartered, and the execution was carried out in the King's presence on the following day, 15 July.[29] His remains, like those of the other rebel leaders, were quartered and sent to the four corners of the kingdom. Having impressed the St Albans townsmen with the grim theatre of royal vengeance, Tresilian and the rest of the royal party set out for Barnet on the following day.[30]

The men of St Albans were left to stew until Tresilian's return on 13 October. During the intervening months, the townsmen had resolved to resist Tresilian, but the Chief Justice soon overcame the juries' reluctance to testify by a mixture of threats and persuasion. Although no friend to the townsmen, Walsingham's views of Tresilian's methods were not entirely favourable. Describing him as 'cunning like a serpent' he related how the indicted men were tried before three separate juries of twelve men. Once the first jury had made its accusations, the second was tricked into condemning the indicted men, while the third was allowed only to see the verdicts and confirm whether they were reliable. In a gross perversion of due process, Tresilian stated proudly that no man in St Albans had been convicted but on the word of thirty-six men. After this show-trial, William Grindecobbe, William Cadendon and John Barbitonsor, together with thirteen others, were dragged to the gallows and hanged. Eighty others were sentenced to imprisonment, including Richard Wallingford, who had acted as a go-between for Tyler and Grindecobbe.[31]

But, even in the face of this brutality, the townsmen were not entirely cowed. A brave individual brought an indictment to Tresilian alleging that Abbot de la Mare had set up the entire revolt in St Albans, and had urged the rebels to go to London. Browbeaten by Tresilian with dire threats, the townsman withdrew his allegation. Even after this, anonymous slanders against Abbot de la Mare were circulated around St Albans.[32]

The proceedings in St Albans reveal a tragic and squalid dimension to the suppression of the revolt. Grindecobbe and his fellow defendants were undoubtedly the victims of a political decision to liquidate the leading St Albans rebels. Tresilian's methods made him many enemies, and he would end his days on the block seven years later when a group of noblemen purged Richard II's court. Ironically, the three leaders of this purge were also men who had played a part in suppressing the Great Rising – Thomas of Woodstock, Earl of Buckingham, the Earl of Arundel (briefly Chancellor after Sudbury's death) and the Earl of Warwick. The contrast between the timidity of the nobility for much of June 1381, and their new-found courage at handing down capital sentences, was not an edifying spectacle. But by the autumn of 1381 these brutal methods of suppression had paid off, and the Rising had been brought to an end.

THE NOVEMBER 1381 PARLIAMENT

Once the judicial inquisitions had been scaled down, England's political *élite* undertook a form of post-mortem (to borrow Dobson's phrase) on all that had happened since the beginning of June. Parliament opened on Monday 4 November 1381 with an oration from Sir Hugh Seagrave, steward of the royal household during the Rising, who had since been advanced to the office of Treasurer of England. In his speech he posed a number of questions about how best the crown and political community should respond to the challenge from the common people. The Commons were then invited to withdraw to Westminster Hall, and debate Seagrave's speech. After several days of discussion, the Commons returned their findings through their Speaker, Sir Richard Waldegrave. A Suffolk landowner, his fellow knights and gentlemen had suffered some of the worst depredations of the Great Rising. When asked by Seagrave for the Commons' response to the King's revocation of the charters of emancipation that he had granted on 14 June, Waldegrave replied that the House wholly supported his actions.

This was the same reactionary attitude of a county squirearchy that had driven the enactment of the Ordinance and Statute of Labourers thirty years before – and would fight to preserve the Corn Laws more than four centuries later. In the response of the Commons it is possible to discern the origins of a distinc -tive county opinion – offloading blame on the royal household for its excessive size, onto the nobility for their protection of their criminous retainers, and to the King's victuallers and purvey-ors for requisitioning their commodities without payment. Unsurprisingly, the knights, gentlemen and prosperous towns-men represented in the Parliamentary Commons saw little to blame in their own collusion to maintain their own standards of living by artificially depressing the wages of their villeins and servants.[33]

Waldegrave then demanded that the King's chief ministers be dismissed, and that more 'sufficient' men be appointed. William Courtenay, who had succeeded Sudbury as Chancellor as well as Archbishop of Canterbury, was dismissed, and a veteran northern lord and knight, Lord Scrope of Bolton, was appointed in his place. Perhaps the House of Commons had become weary of Chancellor-Archbishops, after the catastrophe of the Poll Taxes.

Finally, the Commons requested three general pardons that were duly conceded: the first was to all who had executed rebels without due process, the second to those who had rebelled, and the third to all men who had remained loyal. In his response, Richard agreed, but wanted to withhold his pardon from the men of Bury St Edmunds, Cambridge and Canterbury. In the end, only the men of Bury were excluded from the King's peace – as well as any who had participated in the murders of his ministers, and any who had escaped from gaol during the Rising.[34] But the November Parliament's success as the ceremonial re-assertion of the ruling order belied a feud between two of the kingdom's leading subjects, one that was rapidly threatening to degenerate into private warfare.

JOHN OF GAUNT AND THE EARL OF NORTHUMBERLAND

To understand the origins of the bitter feud between the King's senior uncle and his cousin Henry Percy, it is necessary to return to the opening days of the Rising. Gaunt had been in the north of England at the beginning of June 1381, and had been negotiating a truce with the Scots, in his capacity as Lieutenant of the Marches.[35] Had the Duke been further south, and especially anywhere near London, his life would have been gravely endangered. Constance of Castile, the Duchess of Lancaster, had been in the south or the midlands, and it was perhaps the hatred that was commonly voiced against her husband that caused her to flee into Yorkshire. But, just as the Abbot of Leicester had feared that the Duke's furniture would be a magnet for rebels to attack his own buildings, so the constable of the Duke's own castle of Pontefract refused to admit her, and it was not until she had reached another Lancastrian stronghold, Knaresborough, that she found shelter.[36]

The fact that Gaunt was in Berwick (as far as possible from the centre of the Rising while remaining in England) had serious repercussions for his understanding of the passage of events in the south. On 17 June news from the south finally reached Gaunt, although Simon Walker has concluded that it related to events that had occurred no later than 11 June. That day he issued orders for his castles in Yorkshire and in Wales to be put in a defensible state, and the removal of his household from Leicester to Pontefract.[37] The following day he met King Robert II's son and eventual successor, the Earl of Carrick, whose offer of 20,000 men to defeat the Rising the Duke politely declined.[38] Is it possible that at this stage the Scots were better informed about the scale of events in England than the Duke himself? Gaunt then remained at Berwick for three days, during which time various rumours reached him to the effect that:

> …two packs of the wicked wolves were ranging through the kingdom, one on the eastern side and the other on the western side, and that either pack contained 10,000 men chosen to seize him, and that all that he had in Leicester had been destroyed, and that Tutbury Castle had been attacked…[39]

Not only was all of this untrue, as Henry Knighton himself pointed out, but it also failed to report the Duke's actual losses at the Savoy. The decision to move to the great fortress at Bamburgh Castle, was taken on 20 June, but on the following day the Duke was intercepted by two messengers, Sir John Hothum and Thomas Motherby, who had been sent by the Earl of Northumberland, under whose command Bamburgh lay. The result of this interview was Gaunt's about-turn, and his request for letters of safe conduct from the Earl of Carrick, on 22 June. The following day the Duke, accompanied by a dwindling band of his servants headed by Sir Walter Urswick and Sir John Marmion, crossed into Scotland at Roxburgh, and were subsequently given an honourable reception at Haddington, and then at Holyrood.[40]

Why Gaunt suddenly turned in his tracks after encountering Northumberland's messengers was the root of the conflict between the two men. The chroniclers claim that Percy had sent the messengers to deliberately refuse the Duke access to any castle under his control, and, even more damagingly, to inform him that he had forfeited the favour of the King.[41] But, during the November 1381 Parliament, the two messengers submitted their own testimony of what they had told the Duke. Their message was simply that Northumberland, the Earl of Stafford and the Bishop of Hereford had advised the Duke to remain at Bamburgh, until he had received further details of events in the south.

What remains puzzling is why such an apparently innocent communication could lead to such bad blood between the Earl and the Duke. Beyond the obvious explanation of mutual incomprehension at a time of political stress and confusion, it is possible that Gaunt believed that the obligation on Percy to give him shelter transcended any orders from the royal council in London. Deeper underlying causes for the dispute have also been located in Percy's envy of Gaunt's recent appointment as paramount Lieutenant of the Marches, a position that threatened his status as the leader of political society in the north of the kingdom.[42]

But the real problem lay in the way that both men handled this misunderstanding – which in the end would become more important than the initial cause of their disagreement. After a comfortable sojourn as a guest of Scotland's leading noble families in Edinburgh, Gaunt made a leisurely progress back to London. However, it is difficult to believe that his mood was not affected by the common perception that he had fled to save his skin, and by the prospect of the charred remains of his beloved London residence. Matters came to a head at a session of the royal council on 15 August at Westminster. In spite of the Earl's repeated apologies for any misunderstanding, Gaunt alleged that Northumberland had not only denied him access to provisions, but had also spread rumours that he had been in treasonable confederacy with the Scots. Gauntlets were then thrown down. Although interventions from other councillors prevented the two protagonists from further provocations, this was merely a temporary halt to a serious personality clash. At the next council session, on 9 October at Berkhamsted, Gaunt repeated his allegations, eliciting from the Earl a torrent of verbal abuse in what Walsingham identified as a northern *patois*.

When Parliament opened in November, rumours abounded of impending violence between the two magnates' retinues. Apparently the Londoners exploited the dispute as a vehicle for their hatred of the Duke, and made their sympathies clear in a rapturous welcome for Northumberland. Gaunt arrived with a large retinue in attendance, and lodged at the Bishop of London's manor of Fulham.

After allowing both men to have their say, Richard intervened and took the entire matter into his own grace.[41] This was a considerable challenge for the young King. With the eyes of Parliament upon him, he had to satisfy the honour of two great men who had exchanged words of high disdain, neither of whose honour could countenance a humiliating withdrawal. Whatever the degree of behind-the-scenes assistance that Richard had received in brokering the deal, it was a masterpiece of compromise. Gaunt's ego was salved by Northumberland's apology, which was delivered on bended knee, and addressed him by his pretended title of 'King of Castile':

> ...And, my lord of Spain, whereas at Berkhamsted in the presence of my most redoubtable lord the King, I, by my ignorance,

gave answer otherwise than I should have done to you, my lord, who are son to my redoubtable liege lord the King (i.e. Edward III), whom God absolve, and uncle to my redoubtable liege lord the King, here present, and so high a person and of such very noble and royal blood as you are, my lord. And also to you, my lord, who are the greatest lord and the highest person of the realm after my liege lord the King, here present, and I of your blood and alliance, having thrown down my gauge before you in the presence of my liege lord the King, here present, I beg your pardon and your honourable lordship.

The tone of the apology was clearly to Gaunt's liking, as a transcript was recorded in the ducal *Register*.[42] Then the Earl's innocence of any malicious intent to the Duke was publicised by Thomas Motherby's submission to Parliament of the text of the communication that he and Hothum had delivered. The Earl and the Duke were then publicly reconciled, and exchanged the kiss of peace at the Chancellor's invitation.[45]

If Richard II's handling of this dispute had been an accurate foretaste of his skills in conflict resolution, the later history of his reign might have been very different. But beneath the ephemeral froth of injured egos, the Gaunt-Percy dispute revealed the extent to which the Rising was capable of exacerbating the ever-present, but usually invisible, tensions between two powerful men, whose interests in the north had rubbed together like great tectonic plates, with explosive results.

Although the inquiries and commissions continued well into the following year, the Parliament of November 1381 marked the end of the main phase of the crown's response to the Great Rising. Stability and authority had been restored, but at a high cost in lives, and with much lingering mistrust between all ranks of Englishmen and women. But this ill feeling was not simply confined to hatred on the part of the cowed commons, and fear among the propertied. The evidence from the proceedings of Parliament show that, once the immediate threat of further large scale violence had passed, rival elements within the political community felt confident to break the temporary solidarity that had prevailed since June, and enter into a cycle of blame and recrimination.

ENGLISH POLITICS AFTER 1381

Popular revolt played a surprisingly small role in the turbulent politics of the remaining years of Richard II's reign. This may well have been due to a combination of increasing governmental vigilance, and the enduring effects of the bloody repression of the summer of 1381. But in spite of the undoubted success of the government in restoring order, this did not enable Richard II and his ministers to establish a truly stable foundation for his rule. Throughout the 1380s Richard II and his council were haunted by England's continuing failure to score any successes against France. In 1383 Bishop Despenser led a military expedition into the Low Countries, with the intention of liberating the Flemish manufacturing towns from French rule, and restoring the Count of Flanders, Louis de Male, who had been driven from his lands by rebels supported by Charles VI. But this proved to be no more successful than the interventions in Brittany ten years previously, and the chief result was a humiliating evacuation of Despenser's forces from Flanders in September of that year. This episode gravely tarnished the reputation of the hero of 1381, and he was subsequently impeached on a number of charges, including the failure to appoint sufficiently experienced lay men as his field commanders.[46]

Failings in the French war also destroyed the career of Sir Michael de la Pole, who, with the Earl of Arundel, had been placed in the king's household in November 1381 as a mentor, at the bequest of Parliament. But, far from becoming Parliament's 'man on the inside' of the court, de la Pole became a firm royal favourite, rising to the rank of chancellor and Earl of Suffolk. In 1386, amidst well-founded fears of a French invasion, Parliament impeached de la Pole against Richard II's wishes, and set in train two years of conflict between the King and his courtiers on one side, and his leading enemies and their Parliamentary supporters on the other. De la Pole's impeachment, and the subsequent takeover of government by a Parliament-appointed Commission in the autumn of 1386, pitted Richard II against a group of his leading magnates.[47]

The three most senior supporters of the Commission were Richard II's uncle, Thomas of Woodstock, and the Earls of Arundel and Warwick. John of Gaunt, the only man in England who would have had the personal authority to mediate in this dispute, was pursuing his Castilian ambitions, but his son Henry sided with the Commission and its noble supporters. During 1387 this dispute escalated into open armed conflict, and the eventual result was a vicious series of state trials in Parliament during which a number of Richard II's personal friends and senior ministers were executed or exiled. Michael de la Pole and the King's favourite, Robert de Vere Earl of Oxford, ended their days in French exile, while Sir Simon Burley (the King's former tutor) and Sir Robert Tresilian (the hanging judge of 1381) were beheaded. Although Richard II regained control of government in 1389, he did not forget his treatment at the hands of his own leading noblemen. The royal revenge came unexpectedly in the summer of 1397. In a deliberate imitation of the humiliating state trials that he had co-ordinated in 1388, the Earl of Arundel was condemned as a traitor in full parliament, and beheaded on 21 September 1397. Arrested on royal orders, Thomas of Woodstock was spirited off to a Calais Inn where he was secretly smothered to death after confessing that he had conspired against his royal nephew. The Earl of Warwick did not escape either, and, like Gloucester and Arundel, was stripped of all of his estates before being sentenced to perpetual imprisonment on the Isle of Man.[48]

John of Gaunt had presided over the parliamentary trials of 1397, but otherwise he had avoided close personal entanglement in his nephew's plans for revenge, as his main concerns lay with ensuring the smooth transfer of his estates to his son, Henry, after his death. But Richard was increasingly suspicious of his cousin, and in 1398 his fears were confirmed by a quarrel that broke out between Henry and Thomas Mowbray, Duke of Norfolk. Both men had opposed Richard in the period 1387-8, and it seems that the root of their quarrel was Mowbray's fear that they would soon suffer the same vengeance that the King had meted out to Woodstock and Arundel. In the autumn of 1398, as his reign became increasingly tyrannical, Richard II banished both Henry and Mowbray from the kingdom after an abortive trial by battle. A few months later, in February 1399, Gaunt died and Richard intervened to sequestrate his great inheritance, and decreed that Henry's banishment, initially set at a ten year tariff, should be perpetual.[49]

Richard II's decision to lead a major expedition to Ireland gave Henry the opportunity that he needed, and in July of 1399 he returned from exile, and soon gathered a powerful coalition of lords and barons around him. When Richard returned to his kingdom it became clear that his subjects were not willing to fight for him, and he was eventually forced to surrender into Henry's hands in August 1399. In October 1399 Richard II was deposed by Henry of Lancaster – the man with whom he shared anxious days in The Tower at the height of the 1381 revolt. Richard II's fate was sealed in January 1400, after his supporters had failed in their attempts to assassinate Henry as a forerunner to liberating him from Pontefract castle. It is a measure of the unpopularity of Richard II's cause that the chief architects of the plot were lynched by commoners in Cirencester, Essex and Bristol.[50] But at least one of the leading figures of 1381 survived these tribulations. After his impeachment in 1383 Henry Despenser avoided court politics for many years until the summer of 1399 when, in a characteristic display of exceptionalism, he was the only leading royalist who offered battle to Henry of Lancaster after Richard II's capture. In January 1400 Bishop Despenser was imprisioned again, following rumours of his involvement in the abortive restoration of Richard II (his nephew, Lord Despenser, had been lynched as one of the ringleaders). However, the new king may have appreciated Henry Despenser's spirit, as he was released soon after, and remained bishop of Norwich until his death in 1406.

8

THE RISING IN HISTORY

The ruling elite of the later fourteenth and early fifteenth centuries were not quick to forget the events of 1381. When Richard II learned that the St Albans townsmen had gone to Easthampstead and removed the bodies of their executed fellows from the gibbet, he ordered that they be replaced. Walsingham claimed that in the August heat the townsmen were made to return the 'foetid, verminous and putrid' corpses to their chains.[1]

But was this merely the return to a *status quo ante*, or did the Rising have a longer-term effect on the economy and society of the later middle ages? At first sight, Richard II's revocation of the manumission charters of 14 June marked the failure of the rebels' main demand. However, the King's orders commanding villeins to perform their accustomed services pitted political will against irresistible long-term economic and social trends. The decline of serfdom may have had the pace of a glacier, but it also had its irresistible force. There were, of course, many thousands of men and women who continued to hold their lands as villein tenements, but landholders were increasingly concerned to bolster their stagnant profits by commuting servile dues for cash payments. Those concerned to prevent the migration of their tenants were often willing to change the terms of a tenancy to a leasehold, often lasting for many years. Hilton notes that, by the middle of the fifteenth century many tenants considered themselves to be free on the strengths of their copyhold tenures.[2] Some villeins were freed outright by their lords, and such was the case of William Grey, who was formally 'manumitted' (released from serfdom) by John Fordham, Bishop of Durham, on 25 April 1388.[3]

Not all proprietors were willing to accept the realities of a changing economy. In 1394 the Earl of Warwick went to great lengths to recover a man called David Tregoyse, whom he claimed as a villein of one of his Devon estates, and who had absconded to Saltash. Repeated efforts to secure his indictment before a justice in Cornwall were obstructed by the hidden hand of royal disfavour – three years later the Earl would be banished and forfeit his estates.[4]

Hilton has detected the endurance of some of the tenurial conditions of serfdom on ecclesiastical estates in the early years of the sixteenth century. This is likely to have been straightforward economic exploitation of poor tenants on small holdings, who lacked the mobility or opportunity to seek better conditions. In the revolt of 1549 the demands of Robert Kett's followers included the liberation from villeinage of the tenants of the Howard Dukes of Norfolk.[5] As late as 1575 Elizabeth I's surveyors found a new source of revenue in the anachronistic persistence of villein tenancies on some of the crown estates. She proceeded to sell a total of 300 of her bondsmen and bondswomen to Sir Henry Lee, who was able to profit from their purchases of redemption.[6] It is a quirk of English history that after 1381 there was no great royal order of emancipation, and that the bonds of serfdom disappeared through prolonged immersion in the solvent of economic change.

Just as villeinage endured in various forms after the Great Rising, so protest continued to play a part in the politics of later medieval England. As early as 1382 a conspiracy was uncovered in

Norfolk for the assassination of Bishop Despenser. Betrayed by one of their fellows, the conspirators were beheaded in Norwich, seemingly without trial.[7] A far more serious disturbance broke out in Sussex on the estates of the Earl of Arundel, in 1383, when Lewes Castle was stormed, and its records burned.[8] Resentment against the power of the Fitzalan dynasty had long predated the Great Rising. In 1377 the men of the county had petitioned the new King to withhold from Arundel an annual payment from the county called 'Sheriffgeld', worth nearly £20 annually, that Edward III had granted to his father, the previous Earl.[9]

A major disturbance broke out in Cheshire in 1393, but this cannot really be characterised as social in its objectives, as it was principally a campaign by the county's gentry against the King's diplomatic rapprochement with France. The men of Cheshire had long augmented their incomes through military service. In 1414 the heretical leader Sir John Oldcastle brought several hundred disillusioned men and women into his cause. Mostly these were outsiders, opportunists and misfits.[10] It was not until the Kentish rising of 1450 that a revolt can be found of a comparable scale to that of 1381. Although there are some superficial points of similarity – such as the invasion of London, the slaying of royal ministers, and leadership by a charismatic individual, Jack Cade – the 1450 rising was almost entirely political in its orientation. Resentment against the loss of the war with France, and the activities in the county of hated courtiers, combined to produce a remarkable explosion of violence.[11] Like their forebears of 1381, the Kentishmen took their grievances to London, but their stated objectives were universally political, and driven by their hatred of the men of the royal household. However, the crown feared that there was a strong social component to the rebels' ambitions, and in the Statute of Attainder passed against its leaders in 1452, Jack Cade was described as 'Another imp of Hell and Successor of Wat'.

In 1489 disturbances broke out in Yorkshire against Henry VII's tax-raising. His Lieutenant-general, the Earl of Northumberland, was assassinated not only for his supervision of tax collection, but also due to a widespread resentment against his burgeoning power. Eight years later there was a major rising in Cornwall, once more directed against royal taxation. Although the Cornishmen reached Blackheath (a location of some resonance), Henry VII threw the city into a defensible state, and faced with the King's guns and royal army of 25,000, they lost heart and dispersed.[12]

There were elements of agrarian protest in the religious risings of 1536 and 1549, but these were not really concerned with the condition of tenancies, but rather were the results of the general economic depression and marginalisation (manifested in inflation and enclosure), which were felt by a broad cross-section of Tudor society. If there were points of comparison connecting the later popular revolts with that of 1381, then these may be located not in their causes or objectives, but in the patterns of protest. That rebels returned to Blackheath in 1450 and 1497, and to Mousehold Heath in 1549, was no mere coincidence. I.M.W. Harvey has shown the events of 1381 were preserved in the memories of fifteenth century Englishmen through aphorisms and rhymes, and their penetration of folk memory was such that in 1407, and again in 1485, the leaders of very minor revolts in Warwickshire and north Yorkshire called themselves 'Jack Straw'.[13] Like Robin Hood and his mythical companions, Jack Straw became a recognisable character in England's folk traditions.[14] Lincoln's Inn even had a festive mumming featuring Jack Straw as an unlikely 'King of Christmas' (perhaps a gesture of defiance by the legal apprentices to their masters?) until it was banned in 1519.[15]

The legacy of 1381 gained a new political relevance in the seventeenth century. Some of the more radical Puritan sects saw the English Republic as a mirror of the events of 1381, when Tyler and his fellows had sought to cast off 'The Norman Yoke'. The concept of a state of pre-Norman Conquest English liberty gained wide currency at this time, echoing the faith invested by the men of St Albans and Bury in the charters of the Kings, Offa and Cnut. But

'The Saints' and 'Fifth Monarchy of Men' of the mid-seventeenth century did not enjoy a monopoly of interpretations of the events of 1381.[16] In 1642 Charles I rebuked the 'Nineteen Propositions of Both Houses' demanding rule through Parliament, and expressed his fears that 'this excellently distinguished form of government will end in a dark, equal chaos of confusion, and the long line of our many noble ancestors in a Jack Cade or a Wat Tyler'.[17] An even more hostile voice was that of John Cleveland, an antiquary and historian of Royalist sympathies. In *The Idol of The Clownes* of 1654, Cleveland identified the men of 1381 as part of a continuum of rebellion and sedition, which had come to a poisonous fruition in his own age:

> These were but types of Tyler the Idol, and acted nothing but according to his great example; they were wolves alike, and he that reads one knowes all. Thomas of Becket, Simon of Montfort the English Cataline; Thomas of Lancaster, rebels and traitors of the former years are canonised by the monks (generally the enemies of their kings) miracles make their tombs illustrious, and their memories sacred.[18]

For Cleveland, the leaders of the 1381 revolt stood as symbolic substitutes for Cromwell and the other army leaders. In Cleveland's writings, Tyler 'the future monarch, who had designed an Empire for himselfe' was a thinly disguised Cromwell. This parallel between the rule of army in the counties in the 1650s, and the supposed ambitions of Tyler for a federation of kingdoms, endured into the eighteenth century in works such as *The History of Wat Tyler and Jack Straw, Being a Relation of Their Notorious Rebellion*:

> …wanting a Captain to lead them, they chose a lewd bold Fellow, named Wat, or Walter Tyler, a Taylor (*sic*), a Man whose necessities made him prone to all mischief, and substituted under him his lieutenant general, Jack Straw… and under these they

appointed other officers, as such who headed parties in the counties… appointed to redress the grievances of the Nation, and that they were servants of the Commonwealth of England.[19]

By the eighteenth century the events of 1381 were well-established in the popular street culture of London. The author of *The History of Wat Tyler and Jack Straw* noted that the city of London had an 'Annual Triumphal Show', celebrating the defeat and suppression of the Rising. As Peter Linebaugh notes, by the middle of the century, the stories of Tyler, Straw and Ball had become the subjects for popular plays and burlesques in London's street theatre. Lord George Gordon declined to relinquish the leadership of his move-ment, fearing that 'there might spring up some Wat Tyler who would not have patience to commune with Government, and might very possibly chuse to embroil the nation in civil war'.[20]

As the shock waves of revolutionary France reached England, the legacy of 1381 was contested by Royalists and radicals alike. Edmund Burke, fearing the spread of revolutionary contagion from France, characterised the 1381 Rising as 'a dark age'. Thomas Paine's rejoinder in *The Rights of Man* was forthright:

> Tyler appears to have been an intrepid disinterested man, with respect to himself. All his proposals made to Richard, were on a more just and public ground than those which had been made to John by the barons; and notwithstanding the sycophancy of historians, and men like Mr Burke, who seek to gloss over a base action of the court by traducing Tyler, his fame will outlive their falsehood.[21]

Inspired by Paine's defence of the leaders of 1381, the twenty-year-old Robert Southey wrote a dramatic poem, 'Wat Tyler', which he presented to the Revd Winterbotham, then in Newgate Gaol. But, due to its inflammatory political content, 'Wat Tyler' was formally suppressed by the Lord Chancellor's office, and went unpublished for many years. In 1817 a copy was stolen by radicals, who printed it against the wishes of Southey, who had long since repudiated his radical connections, and had accepted the Poet Laureateship four years previously. In spite of Southey's efforts to obtain an injunction against publication, 'Wat Tyler' was published at 3s 6d, and it was later claimed that upwards of 40,000 copies were sold. Southey's apostasy from the radical cause earned him the condemnation of Lord Byron in 1821, and 'Wat Tyler' was not included in the ten volumes of his work for another fifteen years.[22]

During the later nineteenth century the Great Rising lost much of its potency as a political symbol, and its portrayal was typified by the kitsch *Histerical* (sic) *Burlesque – Wat Tyler: Or, The Prize Fight That was Settled by a Mace*, of 1867. On 20 December 1869 G.A. Sala's appropriately pantomimic *Wat Tyler MP, An Operatic Extravaganza*, opened at the Gaiety Theatre on the Strand. With the advent of the twentieth century, political realism intruded into the literary treatment of the Rising, and Halcot Glover's *Wat Tyler, A Play in Three Acts*, elaborated the events of 1381 from a modern socialist perspective.[23]

The Great Rising of 1381 has remained embedded in the historical consciousness of Britain for more than six centuries. Richard II, John of Gaunt, William Walworth and Wat Tyler remain famous names, even if the understanding of their roles in the events of 1381 has dimmed. John Cleveland felt it necessary to correct the popular misconception that the dagger on the arms of the Corporation of London commemorated Walworth's stabbing of Tyler, whereas in fact it was the sword of St Paul.[24] Such a blurring of detail is not untypical of the transmission to the modern era of our understanding of the Great Rising.

But the events of 1381 have had an undeniable role in shaping popular political discourse. The levelling speeches attributed to John Ball have for centuries inspired rebels and revolutionaries, even if the original context of their delivery has long since been forgotten. The fascination that they have engendered in politicians, rebels, artists and political scientists in subsequent centuries attests to their enduring significance as statements of alienation and dissent.

Wat Tyler, John Ball and the leaders of the county risings were the first ordinary men in the British Isles to mount a credible attack on the political and economic structures of their day. For all the flaws and inconsistencies in their stated objectives, and in the prosecution of their campaign, the rebels of 1381 succeeded in giving a voice to those who had hitherto lacked any means of expressing their common political grievances. In spite of the defeat of its aims and the execution of its leaders, the Great Rising demonstrated that there was a latent political conciousness at all ranks of society. Denied any effective means of political representation, and subject to royal misgovernance and seigniorial oppression, the people of England found a voice for the first time in June 1381. Long after their defeat, the echoes of their cries reverberated in the politics of the English, and later British, states.

A NOTE ON THE SOURCES

Any historian of the Great Rising is indebted to the indispensable collection of sources collated more than thirty years ago by Prof. R.B. Dobson. In most cases I have used the most recently available printed editions of chronicles, but I have also endeavoured to indicate where I have drawn on Prof. Dobson's translations. When establishing a chronology for the Great Rising, I have in most cases followed the dates suggested by Prof. Dobson and by Prof. Caroline Barron in her *Revolt in London: 11 to 15 June*. Finally, the historical understanding of the suppression of the Great Rising is heavily dependent on the ground-breaking doctoral thesis of Prof. A.J. Prescott. Although I have consulted a sample of the judicial records, I have also endeavoured to indicate where I have made use of Prof. Prescott's findings.

ABBREVIATIONS

Anon. Chron.: The Anonimalle Chronicle, 1333-81 ed. V.H. Galbraith (Manchester, 1927).

BL: British Library.

CCR: Calendar of Close Rolls.

CFR: Calendar of Fine Rolls.

CPR: Calendar of Patent Rolls.

Dobson, *Peasants' Revolt*: R.B. Dobson, ed., *The Peasants' Revolt of 1381* (2nd edn Macmillan, London, 1983).

EHR: English Historical Review.

Froissart, *Chronicles*: Jean Froissart, *Chronicles,* ed. T. Johnes, 2 vols (*Rolls Series*, London 1868).

Hist. Angl.: Historia Anglicana, ed. H.T. Riley, 2 vols (*Rolls Series*, London, 1863-4).

Knighton's Chron.: Knighton's Chronicle 1337-1396, ed. G.H. Martin (Oxford, 1995).

NA: PRO: The National Archives (Public Record Office).

Westm. Chron.: The Westminster Chronicle 1381-1394, ed. L.C. Hector and B.F. Harvey (Oxford, 1982).

NOTES

I THE RURAL WORLD OF THE FOURTEENTH CENTURY

1. C.C. Dyer, *Everyday Life in Medieval England* (London, 1994), 200-202.
2. G.C. Homans, *English Villagers of the Thirteenth Century* (New York, 1970), 18-22.
3. Dyer, *Everyday Life in Medieval England*, 141-3, 151.
4. Homans, *English Villagers of the Thirteenth Century*, 75.
5. Dyer, *Everyday Life in Medieval England*, 134.
6. *Idem, Standards of Living in the Late Middle Ages: Social Change in England, c.1200-1520* (Cambridge, 1989), 119.
7. P. Vinogradoff, *Villainage in England, Essays in English Medieval History* (2nd ed., Oxford, 1968), 143-8.
8. J. Hatcher, 'English serfdom and villeinage: towards a re-assessment', *Landlords, Peasants and Politics in Medieval England*, ed. T.H. Aston (Cambridge, 1987), 250-1.
9. P.R. Hyams, *Kings, Lords and Peasants in Medieval England, The Common Law of Villeinage in the Twelfth and Thirteenth Centuries* (Oxford, 1980), 2-30.
10. *Ibid.*, 125-31
11. Vinogradoff, *Villeinage in England*, 354.
12. *Ibid.*, 279-87.
13. M. Morgan, *The English Lands of The Abbey of Bec* (Oxford, 1946), 79.
14. R.H. Hilton, *A Medieval Society: The West Midlands at the End of the Thirteenth Century* (Cambridge, 1966), 139.
15. Hyams, *Kings, Lords and Peasants*, 168-79.
16. NA: PRO Durham 3/30 (1353-4), m.19.
17. Hyams, *Kings, Lords and Peasants*, 206.
18. Z. Razi, *Life, Marriage and Death in a Medieval Parish* (Cambridge,1980), 31; *Hist. Angl.* i, 147.
19. J. Hatcher, *Plague, Population and the English Economy* (London, 1977), 68.
20. Razi, *Life, Marriage and Death in a Medieval Parish*, 94-8.
21. R.H. Hilton, *A Medieval Society, The West Midlands at the End of the Thirteenth Century* (Cambridge, 1966), 147.
22. R.R. Davies, *The Revolt of Owain Glyn Dwr* (Oxford, 1995), 65-70.

23. E. Miller and J. Hatcher, *Medieval England – Rural Society and Economic Change 1086-1348* (London, 1978), 45.

24. Miller and Hatcher, *Rural Society and Economic Change*, 50-1.

25. *Ibid*, 68.

26. C. Dyer, *Standards of Living In the Later Middle Ages: Social Change in England* (Cambridge, 1989), 157-9.

27. C.M. Woolgar, 'Conspicuous Consumption and the Diet of the Nobility in the Fifteenth Century', *Revolution and Consumption in Late Medieval England*, ed. M. Hicks (Boydell, Woodbridge, 2001), 16-17.

28. NA: PRO Just. Itin. 1/947/6 (1).

29. Dyer, *Standards of Living*, 154.

30. J.L. Bolton, *The Medieval English Economy, 1150-1500* (London, 1980), 182-3.

31. J.R. Maddicott, *The English Peasantry and Demands of the Crown* (*Past & Present Supplement*, Oxford, 1975), 4-5, 6-15.

32. R. Horrox, ed. *The Black Death* (Manchester, 1994), 235.

33. P.D.A. Harvey, *A Medieval Village, Cuxham, 1240-1400* (Oxford, 1965), 135; R.H. Britnell, *The Commercialisation of English Society, c.1000-1500* (Cambridge, 1989), 156.

34. Horrox, *Black Death*, 238; E.B. Fryde, *Peasants and Landlords in Later Medieval England c.1380–c.1520* (Stroud, 1996), 32–3.

35. Britnell, *Commercialisation of English Society*, 157.

36. G.L. Harriss, *King, Parliament and Public Finance in Medieval England to 1369* (Oxford, 1975), chps 10 and 11.

37. R.C. Palmer, *English Law in the Age of the Black Death, 1348-1381, A Transformation of Governance and Law* (Univ. of N. Carolina Press, Chapel Hill, 1993), 17.

38. *Ibid*, 18.

39. B.H. Puttnam, *The Enforcement of the Statutes of Labourers During the First Decade after the Black Death, 1349-1359* (Columbia Univ. Press, 1908), 69-70.

40. A. Musson, 'New Labour Laws, New Remedies?', *Fourteenth Century England*, i, ed. N. Saul (Woodbridge, 2001), 75-9.

41. Puttnam, *Enforcement of the Statute of Labourers*, 265-6; E.B. Fryde, *Peasants and Landlords in Later Medieval England*, 35.

42. Puttnam, *Enforcement of the Statute of Labourers*, 125, 177-80.

43. Oxfordshire County Record Office M2/D/62.

44. R.H. Hilton, *The Decline of Serfdom in Medieval England* (2nd ed., London, 1977), 44, 49.

45. *The Peasant Land Market in Medieval England*, ed. P.D.A. Harvey (Oxford, 1984), 344.

46. A. Mcfarlane, *The Origins of English Individualism* (Oxford, 1978), 105.

47. R.H. Britnell, 'Feudal Reaction After the Black Death in the Palatinate of Durham', *Past & Present*, 128 (1990), 32-5, 45, 47.

48. G.C. Coulton, *Medieval Village, Manor and Monastery* (New York, 1980), 132–5.
49. *Gesta Abbatum Monasterii Sancti Albani*, ii (*Rolls Series*, London, 1867), 157–168.
50. R. Faith, 'The "Great Rumour" of 1377 and Peasant Ideology', *The English Revolt of 1381*, ed. R.H. Hilton and T.H. Aston (Cambridge, 1984) 43–73.

2 WAR AND PEACE: ENGLAND 1377–81

1. D. Green, *The Black Prince* (Stroud, 2001), 90–2; E. Perroy, *The Hundred Years' War* (London, 1959), 150–7.
2. For summaries, see A. Curry, *The Hundred Years' War* (Basingstoke, 1993) 65–79; C. Allmand, *The Hundred Years' War* (Cambridge, 1989), 20–4.
3. E. Perroy, *The Hundred Years' War*, 158–61.
4. Froissart, *Chronicles*, I, 401–2.
5. *Ibid.*, 419.
6. J. Sherborne, *War, Politics and Culture in Fourteenth-Century England*, ed. J.A. Tuck, 3–5.
7. *Ibid.*, 421–2; A. Goodman, *John of Gaunt*, 229–30.
8. Goodman, *John of Gaunt*, 231.
9. Froissart, *Chronicles*, I, 435.
10. *Ibid.*, 457.
11. Sherborne, *War, Politics and Culture in Fourteenth-Century England*, 6–7.
12. *Ibid.*, 43–4.
13. *Ibid.*, 48–9.
14. M.C.E. Jones, *Ducal Brittany, 1364-1399, Relations with England and France in the reign of Duke John IV* (Oxford, 1970), 62.
15. *Ibid.*, 69.
16. *Ibid.*, 73–6.
17. G.A. Holmes, *The Good Parliament* (Oxford, 1975), 109.
18. Sherborne, *War, Politics and Culture in Fourteenth-Century England*, 12.
19. Goodman, *John of Gaunt*, 233.
20. Sherborne, *War, Politics and Finance in Fourteenth-Century England*, 58.
21. Jones, *Ducal Brtittany*, 80; A. Curry, *The Hundred Years' War* (Basingstoke, 1993), 78.
22. C. Allmand, *The Hundred Years' War, England and France at War, c.1300-c.1450* (Cambridge, 1988), 25.
23. N. Saul, *Richard II* (Yale, 1997), 30–34.
24. A. Goodman, *The Loyal Conspiracy* (London, 1971), 122–3.
25. *Idem, John of Gaunt, The Exercise of Princely Power in Europe* (London, 1992), 73.
26. Saul, *Richard II*, 39–40.

27. Jones, *Ducal Brittany*, 88; Saul, *Richard II*, 43-4.
28. J. Sherborne, *War, Politics and Finance in Fourteenth Century England*, ed. A. Tuck (London, 1994), 68.
29. Goodman, *Loyal Conspiracy*, 123-6; Saul, *Richard II*, 53.
30. *Rolls of Parliament*, iii, 101-3.
31. G.A. Holmes, *The Good Parliament* (Oxford, 1975), 68-9.
32. *Ibid*, 103-5.
33. *Ibid*, 106-7.
34. *Chronicon Angliae 1328-1388*, ed. E. M. Thompson (*Rolls Series*, 1874), 105.
35. William Langland, *Piers Plowman*, ll. 145-58.
36. *Chronicon Angliae*, 92-3; Goodman, *John of Gaunt*, 60.
37. *Chronicon Angliae*, 114-116; Goodman, *John of Gaunt*, 60.
38. *Chronicon Angliae*, 120-7.
39. Goodman, *John of Gaunt*, 62-63.
40. *Chronicon Angliae*, 150, 165.
41. A. Goodman, 'Richard II's Councils', in *Richard II: The Art of Kingship* (Oxford, 1999), 67-9.
42. A. Tuck, *Richard II and the English Nobility* (London, 1973), 39-41.
43. *Chronicon Angliae*, 210-11; Goodman, *John of Gaunt*, 73.
44. W.M. Ormrod, *The Reign of Edward III, Crown and Political Society in England, 1372–1377* (Yale, 1990), 34-5; E.B. Fryde, *Peasants and Landlords in Late Medieval England, c. 1380–1525*, 43.
45. *Rolls of Parliament*, ii, 363-4; *Hist. Angl.*, i, 323-4; Dobson, *Peasants' Revolt*, 103-5.
46. Fryde, *Peasants and Landlords*, 44.
47. *Ibid*.
48. Dobson, *Peasants' Revolt*, 111.
49. *Ibid*, 113.
50. C. Oman, *The Great Revolt of 1381* (New York, 1969), 24-7; Fryde, *Peasants and Landlords*, 44.
51. Local Government Finance Act 1988 (*c*.41); J. Smith and I. Maclean, 'The UK Poll Tax and The Declining Electoral Roll: Unintended Consequences?' *Warwick Economic and Social Research Papers*, 398 (1992), 20-21, 31-3.
52. Oman, *The Great Revolt of 1381*, 162-3, 27-9.
53. CPR 1377-81, 627-8; Saul, *Richard II*, 57.
54. CFR 1377-83, 250; Oman, *Great Revolt*, 29; Saul, *Richard II*, 57.

3 THE REBELS AND THEIR AIMS

1. *Hist. Angl.*, ii, 9-11.
2. *Anon. Chron.*, 139.
3. *Hist. Angl., I*, 468; Dobson, *Peasants' Revolt*, 270.

4. C. Hill, 'The Norman Yoke' in *Puritanism and Revolution* (Pimlico, London, 2001) 44-6; A. Dunn, 'The Many Roles of Wat Tyler', *History Today*, 51 no. 7 (July, 2001) 28-9.

5. *Knighton's Chron.*, 211.

6. *Hist. Angl.*, ii, 34-5.

7. *Knighton's Chron.*, 222-3.

8. For a scholarly analysis of the letters, see R.F. Green, 'John Ball's Letters' in *Chaucer's England*, ed. B.A. Hanawalt (Minnesota, 1992) ch. 9.

9. *Knighton's Chron.*, 243; Dobson, *Peasants' Revolt*, 373.

10. *Hist. Angl.*, i, 458; *Knighton's Chron.*, 218.

11. F.W.D. Brie, 'Wat Tyler and Jack Straw', *EHR*, xxi (1906), 106-11.

12. *Knighton's Chron.*, 216-7; *Hist. Angl.*, i, 454.

13. H. Eiden, 'Joint Action against "Bad" Lordship: The Peasants' Revolt in Essex and Norfolk', *History* 83, no.269 (1998), 25-7.

14. W. M. Ormrod, 'The Politics of Pestilence: Government in England after the Black Death', *The Black Death in England*, ed. W. M. Ormrod and P. Lindley (Stamford, 1996), 159.

15. Hilton, *Bondmen Made Free*, 187.

16. CPR 1381-5, 30-1.

17. Oman, *Great Revolt*, 206-213; Dobson, *Peasants' Revolt*, 213, 220-223.

18. B. Wilkinson, 'The Peasants' Revolt of 1381', *Speculum*, xv (1940), 14-15.

19. R.B. Dobson, 'The Risings in York, Beverley and Scarborough', in *The English Revolt of 1381*, ed. Hilton and Aston, 112-142. C.D. Liddy, 'Urban Conflict in Late-Fourteenth Century England: The Case of York in 1380-1', EHR cxviii (February 2003), 1-32.

20. Dobson, *Peasants' Revolt,* 162; Fryde, *Great Revolt of 1381*, 23; Saul, *Richard II*, 68n.

21. *Anon. Chron.*, 144-5.

22. Dobson, *Peasants' Revolt*, 168; R. Faith, 'The "Great Rumour" of 1377 and Peasant Ideology', 48.

23. Hallam, *Domesday Book*, 38; Fryde, *The Great Revolt*, 24.

24. A. Harding, 'The Revolt against the Justices', in *The English Rising of 1381*, ed. Hilton and Aston, 166.

25. *Anon. Chron.*, 146-7.

26. *Hist. Angl.*, i, 464; ii, 9-10.

27. J. Frazer, *The Golden Bough, A Study in Magic and Religion* (abridged edn, London, 1974), ch. xxv.

4 THE OUTBREAK: 10-13 JUNE

1. Saul, *Richard II*, 57.

2. Barron, *Revolt in London*, 1; *Anon. Chron.*, 134.

3. *Anon. Chron.*, 135; Saul, *Richard II*, 57.

4. NA: PRO KB 9/166/2, m.4.
5. KB 9/166/2, m. 5.
6. A.J. Prescott, 'Judicial Records of The Rising of 1381', (Univ. of London PhD Thesis, 1984), 373-4.
7. Dobson, *Peasants' Revolt*, 126 and 126n; N. Brooks, 'The Organisation and Achievements of The Peasants of Kent and Essex in 1381', 256.
8. H.E.J. Collins, *The Order of The Garter, 1348-1461: Chivalry and Politics in Late Medieval England*, 291.
9. For grants to Burley see Saul, *Richard II*, 112-17.
10. *Anon. Chron.*, 136; N. Brooks, 'The Organisation and Achievements of the Peasants of Kent and Essex in 1381', 267.
11. Froissart, *Chronicles*, i, 654.
12. Prescott, 'Judicial Records of The Rising of 1381', 141.
13. *Anon. Chron.*, 137; N. Brooks, 'The Organization and Achievements of the Peasants of Kent and Essex in 1381', 258.
14. *Anon. Chron.*, 135-7.
15. N. Brooks, 'The Organization and Achievements of The Peasants of Kent and Essex in 1381', 264.
16. NA: PRO KB 9/43, mm.24/2; m.10 (Inquisition at Maidstone, 4-5 July 1381).
17. NA: PRO KB 9/43, mm. 14, 9.
18. A.F. Butcher, 'English Urban Society and the Revolt of 1381', in *The English Rising of 1381*, ed. Hilton and Aston, 107.
19. *Anon. Chron.*, 135; *Hist. Angl.*, i, 454; Froissart, *Chronicles*, i, 654; Oman, *Great Revolt*, 45.
20. *Anon. Chron.*, 138-9.
21. Goodman, *John of Gaunt*, 73; Barron, *Revolt in London*, 2.
22. Froissart, *Chronicles*, i, 656, *Anon. Chron.*, 139-40.
23. G.A. Williams, *Medieval London, From Commune to Capital* (London, 1963), 125.
24. D.J.J. Johnson, *Southwark and the City* (Corporation of London, Oxford, 1969), 24, 70-71.
25. Given-Wilson, *The Royal Household and the King's Affinity*, 50-51.
26. *Anon. Chron.*, 140.
27. *Westm. Chron.* 1-3.
28. NA: PRO KB 9/166, m. 3.
29. Goodman, *John of Gaunt*, 304, 322n.
30. *Hist. Angl.*, i, 457.
31. *Knighton's Chron.*, 215.
32. *Anon. Chron.* 142-3; *Westm. Chron.*, 5; *Hist. Angl.*, i, 457.
33. *Hist. Angl.*, i, 457; following Dobson, *Peasants' Revolt*, 169-70.
34. *Westm. Chron.*, 5.
35. NA: PRO KB 9/43, m.12.
36. *Knighton's Chron.*, 215; *Anon. Chron.* 142.

37. Walker, *Lancastrian Affinity*, 96n; Barron, *Revolt in London*, 4; Goodman, *John of Gaunt*, 308, 322n.
38. CPR 1381-5, 124.
39. John Capgrave, *Chronicle*, 237; *Anon. Chron.*, 142. Some doubt remains as to what a 'quest-monger' did.
40. Barron, *Revolt in London*, 6.
41. KB 9/43, m.10.
42. *Knighton's Chron.*, 211; *Hist. Angl.*, i, 458.
43. *Anon. Chron.*, 143.
44. *Hist. Angl.*, i, 458-9; *Anon. Chron.*, 142-3.

5 THE KING AND THE REBELS

1. B. Wilkinson, 'The Peasants' Revolt of 1381', *Speculum*, xv (1940), 20–24; Dobson, *Peasants' Revolt*, 159.
2. *Knighton's Chron.*, 213.
3. *Anon. Chron.*, 144-5; *Westm. Chron.*, 7; *Knighton's Chron.*, 213; *Hist. Angl.*, I, 462-3; Dobson, *Peasants' Revolt*, 161n.
4. *Anon. Chron.*, 144.
5. *Knighton's Chron.*, 213; *Westm. Chron.*, 7.
6. *Hist. Angl.*, i, 467.
7. B. Harvey, 'Draft Letters of Manumission and Pardon to the Men of Somerset in 1381', *EHR*, lxxx (1965), 89-91; Barron, *Revolt in London*, 5.
8. E.B. Fryde, *The Great Revolt of 1381*, 22.
9. *Anon. Chron.*, 145.
10. *Westm. Chron.*, 7.
11. *Hist. Angl.*, i, 459; Dobson, *Peasants' Revolt*, 172.
12. Froissart, *Chronicles*, i, 659; Barron, *Revolt in London*, 6; *Anon. Chron.*, 144-5; *Hist. Angl.*, i, 460.
13. *Hist. Angl.*, i, 460-1; following Dobson, *Peasants' Revolt*, 173-5.
14. *Knighton's Chron.*, 215; Barron, *The Revolt in London*, 6; *Westm. Chron.*, 7.
15. C. Wilson, 'The Medieval Monuments', *A History of Canterbury Cathedral*, ed. P. Collinson, N. Ramsay and M. Sparks (Oxford, 1995), 471, 472n.
16. Barron, *Revolt in London*, 6.
17. *Anon. Chron.*, 146; Barron, *The Revolt in London*, 7.
18. *Anon. Chron.*, 146; *Westm. Chron.*, 11; Saul, *Richard II*, 70.
19. *Anon. Chron.*, 146; Goodman, *John of Gaunt*, 79; NA: PRO KB 9/166/2, m.2 (Inquisition at Havering-atte-Bower, 26 June 1381).
20. Saul, *Richard II*, 71.
21. Froissart, *Chronicles*, i, 662; *Anon. Chron.*, 146; *Hist. Angl.*, i, 463; Saul, *Richard II*, 70.
22. *Anon. Chron.*, 147; following Dobson, *Peasants' Revolt*, 164.

23. *Anon. Chron.*, 145-6.
24. *Hist. Angl.*, i, 464.
25. *Westm. Chron.*, 11.
26. *Anon. Chron.*, 147-8.
27. *Knighton's Chron.*, 219.
28. Barron, *Revolt in London*, 8.
29. *Hist. Angl.*, i, 464-5; Froissart, *Chronicles*, I, 662; *Westm. Chron.*, 11; *Anon. Chron.*, 148.
30. *Westm. Chron.*, 11; *Knighton's Chron.*, 22; *Anon. Chron.*, 148; *Hist. Angl.*, i, 465; Froissart, *Chronicles*, i, 662; Barron, *Revolt in London*, 8; Saul, *Richard II*, 71.
31. Dobson, *Peasants' Revolt*, 166; Barron, *Revolt in London*, 8.
32. Saul, *Richard II*, 70-1.

6 THE COUNTY RISINGS

1. Brooks, 'The Organisation of the Peasants in Kent and Essex in 1381', 248.
2. D. Crook, 'Derbyshire and the English Rising of 1381', *Historical Research*, lx, no. 141 (1987), 8-12.
3. *Rotuli Parliamentorum*, iii, 96-7. C.D. Liddy, 'Urban Conflict in Late-Fourteenth Century England: The Case of York In 1380-1', 1-32.
4. Dobson, *Peasants' Revolt*, 279-80.
5. A. Gransden, *Historical Writing in Fourteenth Century England*, ii, 123.
6. A. Réville, *Etude sur le Soulèvement de 1381 dans les Comtés de Hertford, de Suffolk et de Norfolk* (Paris, 1898), 7-8.
7. *Gesta Abbatum Monasterii Sancti Albani*, ii, 146-54.
8. *Ibid*, 173-5.
9. *Ibid*, 226-7.
10. *Ibid*, 217-8; Gransden, *Historical Writing in England*, ii, 119.
11. B.L. Cotton Nero D VII, f. 101; Gransden, *Historical Writing in England*, ii, 123.
12. *Gesta Abbatum*, iii, 296-7.
13. B.L. Cotton Nero D VII, f. 109; A. Goodman, *The Loyal Conspiracy*, 149.
14. *Gesta Abbatum*, iii, 298. I am also grateful to Tony Goodman for sharing his thoughts on Thomas Walsingham and St Albans.
15. *Ibid*, 299.
16. *Ibid*, 300.
17. *Ibid*, 300-1.
18. *Ibid*, 303.
19. *Ibid*, 304.
20. *Ibid*, 308-9.
21. Réville, *Etude sur le Soulèvement de 1381*, 22.

22. *Gesta Abbatum*, iii, 319-20.
23. E.P. Thompson, *Customs in Common* (London, 1991), ch. 3.
24. *Gesta Abbatum*, iii, 335.
25. *Ibid*, 336-7.
26. Gransden, *Historical Writing in England*, ii, 168; Goodman, *John of Gaunt*, 79.
27. *Knighton's Chron.*, 231-3.
28. Gransden, *Historical Writing in England*, ii, 168.
29. Oman, *Great Revolt*, 102-3.
30. Powell, *Rising in East Anglia*, 10-11.
31. R.S. Gottfried, Bury St Edmunds and the Urban Crisis, 1290-1535 (New Jersey, 1982), 233.
32. For further details on the laws restricting papal appointments in England, see P. Heath, *Church and Realm, 1272-1461* (Fontana, London, 1988), 129-31.
33. Powell, *Rising in East Anglia*, 16-17; Oman, *Great Revolt*, 106.
34. Powell, *Rising in East Anglia*, 16-17; *Hist. Angl.*, ii, 2.
35. Powell, *Rising in East Anglia*, 13; A.J. Prescott, 'Judicial Records of the Rising of 1381' (Univeristy of London, PhD thesis, 1984), 49.
36. *Hist. Angl.*, ii, 3; Oman, *Great Revolt*, 107.
37. Oman, *Great Revolt*, 109.
38. *Ibid*; Powell, *Rising in East Anglia*, 21.
39. Powell, *Rising in East Anglia*, 25.
40. C. Dyer, 'The Rising of 1381 in Suffolk', in *Everyday Life in Medieval England* (Hambledon and London, 1994), 228-30, 233.
41. Oman, *Great Revolt*, 122-3.
42. D.R. Leader, *A History of the University of Cambridge, i, The University to 1546* (Cambridge University Press, 1988), 87-88.
43. H.P. Stokes, *University of Cambridge, College Histories, Corpus Christi* (F.E. Robinson, London, 1898), 28-9.
44. *Rolls of Parliament*, iii, 108; Powell, *Rising in East Anglia*, 51; Oman, *Great Revolt*, 126.
45. *Hist. Angl.*, ii, 5; Oman, *Great Revolt*, 128.
46. *Hist. Angl.*, ii, 5; Dobson, *Peasants' Revolt*, 257.
47. H. Eiden, 'Joint Action Against "Bad" Lordship: The Peasants' Revolt in Essex and Norfolk', 16-17.
48. *Ibid.*, 18-19.
49. *Ibid.*, 16, 19
50. E. Powell, *The Rising in East Anglia in 1381* (Cambridge, 1896), 28-9.
51. H. Eiden, 'Joint Action against "Bad" Lordship: The Peasants' Revolt in Essex and Norfolk', 20; For the details of the 1549 rising see A. Fletcher, *Tudor Rebellions* (3rd ed., Longman, London, 1983), 54-68.
52. Froissart, *Chronicles*, I, 661; *Hist. Angl.*, ii, 5; Dobson, *Peasants' Revolt*, 261-2.
53. Powell, *Rising in East Anglia*, 30.

54. *Hist. Angl.*, ii, 5-6; M. McKisack, *The Fourteenth Century 1307-1399* (Oxford, 1959), 420-2.

55. H. Eiden, 'Joint Action against "Bad" Lordship: The Peasants' Revolt in Essex and Norfolk', 21

56. *Hist. Angl.*, ii, 6-8, following Dobson, *Peasants' Revolt*, 260.

57. John Capgrave, *Liber de Illustribus Henricis*, ed. F. C. Hingeston (Rolls Series, London, 1858), 172.

58. H. Eiden, 'Joint Action against "Bad" Lordship: The Peasants' Revolt in Essex and Norfolk', 21.

7 THE AFTERMATH

1. R.H.C. Davis, *King Stephen* (London, 1967), ch. 5; D.A. Carpenter, *The Minority of Henry III*, ch. 2 (London, 1990);
J.C. Davies, 'The Despenser War in Glamorgan', *Transactions of The Royal Historical Society* (1915), 21-64.

2. W. M. Ormrod, 'The Peasants' Revolt and the Government of England', *Journal of British Studies*, 29, no. 1 (1990), 8-9.

3. J.A. Tuck, 'Nobles, Commons and the Great Revolt of 1381', in *The English Rising of 1381*, ed. Hilton and Aston, 195-8.

4. CPR 1381-5, 18, 23, 69, 70.

5. CCR 1381-5, 74.

6. A.J. Prescott, 'Judicial Records of the Rising of 1381', (Univ. of London PhD thesis, 1984), 73.

7. NA: PRO KB 9/43 (Inquisition at Maidstone, 4-5 July 1381).

8. Prescott, 'Judicial Records of the Rising of 1381', 46-51.

9. NA: PRO KB 145/3/6/1 (Un-numbered bundle of indictments and trial proceedings for 1381-2).

10. Goodman, *The Loyal Conspiracy*, 96, 99-100.

11. *Hist. Angl.*, ii, 18-19.

12. NA: PRO KB 9/166/2, mm. 1-2.

13. *Ibid*, mm. 4-5.

14. A.J. Prescott, 'Judicial Records of The Rising of 1381', 56.

15. W.H.B. Bird, 'The Peasant Rising of 1381; The King's Itinerary', *EHR*, xxi (1916) 124-5.

16. R. Holt, 'Thomas of Woodstock and Events at Gloucester in 1381', *Bulletin of the Institute of Historical Research*, lviii (1985), 238.

17. CPR 1381-5, 25; For details of the risings in York and Scarborough, see R.B. Dobson, 'The Risings in York, Beverley and Scarborough, 1380-1381', in *The English Rising of 1381*, ed.
Hilton and Aston, 112-42; Prescott, 'Judicial Records of The Rising of 1381', 74. Prescott notes that, shortly afterwards, Northumberland's appointment was superseded by another order appointing a general commission.

18. J.G. Bellamy, *The Law of Treason in England in The Late Middle Ages* (Cambridge, 1970), 103.

19. Prescott, 'Judicial Records of The Rising of 1381', 110-11.

20. *Ibid*, 114-16, 253-8, 292.

21. H. Eiden, 'Joint Action against "Bad" Lordship: The Peasants' Revolt in Essex and Norfolk', 14.

22. *Ibid*, 260, 356.

23. *Hist. Angl.*, ii, 18, following Dobson, *Peasants' Revolt*, 311.

24. *Hist. Angl.*, ii, 10.

25. Réville, *Etude sur le Soulèvement de 1381*, 175-82.

26. *Gesta Abbatum*, iii, 340-7.

27. Prescott, 'Judicial Records of the Rising of 1381', 50-1.

28. *Gesta Abbatum*, iii, 347.

29. *Hist. Angl.*, ii, 34.

30. W.H.B. Bird, 'The Peasant Rising of 1381; The King's Itinerary', *EHR*, xxi (1916) 124-5.

31. *Gesta Abbatum*, iii, 347; *Hist. Angl.*, ii, 35-6; Prescott, 'Judicial Records of The Rising of 1381', 55-7.

32. *Hist. Angl.*, ii, 36-7.

33. *Rolls of Parliament*, iii, 98-103.

34. *Ibid*, 101; Saul, *Richard II*, 81.

35. R.L. Storey, 'The Wardens of The Marches of England Towards Scotland, 1377-1489', *E.H.R.*, lxxii (1957), 596-7.

36. *Knighton's Chron.*, 231.

37. S. Walker, 'Letters to the Dukes of Lancaster in 1381 and 1399', *EHR*, cvi (1991) 69-70.

38. Goodman, *John of Gaunt*, 80.

39. *Knighton's Chron.*, 233.

40. Goodman, *John of Gaunt*, 82.

41. *Anon. Chron.*, 151-2; Froissart, *Chronicles*, I, 665-6.

42. Walker, 'Letters to the Dukes of Lancaster in 1381 and 1399', 68, 72.

43. *Anon. Chron.*, 156.

44. *John of Gaunt's Register, 1379-1383*, ed. E.C. Lodge and R. Somerville, no. 1243. The dispute between Gaunt and Northumberland has now been addressed in detail by K. Towson in 'Hearts warped by Passion: The Percy-Gaunt Dispute of 1381', *Fourteenth Century England*, iii, ed. W.M. Ormrod (Woodbridge, 2003), 143-53. This account is indebted to Towson.

45. *Rolls of Parliament*, iii, 98; Goodman, *John of Gaunt*, 89-90.

46. M. Aston, 'The Impeachment of Bishop Despenser', *Bulletin of The Institute of Historical Research,* xxxvii, no. 98 (1965), 127-48.

47. N. Saul, *Richard II*, chapter eight.

48. *Ibid.*, chapter fifteen; C. Given-Wilson, ed., *Chronicles of The Revolution, 1397-1400, The Reign of Richard II* (Manchester, 1993), 14-24.

49. Given-Wilson, ed., *Chronicles of The Revolution*, 22-5.
50. *Ibid.*, 46-51.

8 THE RISING IN HISTORY

1. *Gesta Abbatum*, iii, 355.
2. R.H. Hilton, *The Decline of Serfdom in Medieval England* (London, 1977), 44-5, 47.
3. NA: PRO Durham 3/32, m.3.
4. NA: PRO SC 8/22/1055.
5. A. Fletcher, *Tudor Rebellions*, 65.
6. Hilton, *Decline of Serfdom in Medieval England*, 50-1.
7. *Hist. Angl.*, ii, 70-1.
8. Oman, *Great Revolt*, 155.
9. NA: PRO SC 8/139/6941.
10. C. Allmand, *Henry V* (California, 1992), 294-305.
11. I.M.W. Harvey, *Jack Cade's Rebellion of 1450* (Oxford, 1991), ch. 2.
12. Fletcher, *Tudor Rebellions*, 11-13.
13. I. M. W. Harvey, 'Was There Popular Politics in Fifteenth-Century England?', *The McFarlane Legacy: Studies in Late Medieval Politics and Society*, ed. R.H. Britnell and A. J. Pollard (Stroud, 1995), 168.
14. For the development and mutation of the Robin Hood legends, see J.C. Holt, Robin Hood (London, 1982).
15. C. Humphrey, *The Politics of Carnival, Festive Misrule in Medieval England* (Manchester, 2001), 49.
16. A. Dunn, 'The Many Roles of Wat Tyler', 28-9.
17. J.P. Kenyon, *The Stuart Constitution, 1603-1688* (Cambridge, 1969), 21.
18. John Cleveland, *The Idol of The Clownes, or The Insurrections of Wat Tyler, With his Priests Baal and Straw* (London, 1654), 1.
19. Anon., *The Garland of Good-Will: Divided Into Three Parts, Containing Many Songs and Poems* (London, c.1700), 4.
20. P. Linebaugh, *The London Hanged* (London, 1991), 347.
21. Thomas Paine, *The Rights of Man, Common Sense and Other Political Writings*, ed. M. Philip (Oxford, 1998), 284.
22. *Five Romantic Plays, 1768-1821*, ed. P. Baines and E. Burns (Oxford, 2000), xiv-xvii.
23. *Wat Tyler: Or, The Prize Fight That Was Settled by a Mace, by D. S., An "Histerical" Burlesque* (London, 1867); G.A. Sala, *Wat Tyler MP, An Operatic Extravaganza*, in *Pantomime and Burlesques*, ii(n.d.); H. Glover, *Wat Tyler, A Play in Three Acts* (c.1920s).
24. Cleveland, *The Idol of The Clownes*, 74.

BIBLIOGRAPHY

PRIMARY SOURCES

(I) MANUSCRIPT SOURCES

NA:PRO
Just. Itin. 1 – Itinerant Justices.
KB 9 – Ancient Indictments.
KB 145 – Indictments and commissions relating to 1381.
SC 8 – Ancient Petitions.
Durham 3 – Chancery Rolls of Palatinate of Durham

BRITISH LIBRARY
Cotton Nero D VII *The Benefactors' Book of St Albans Abbey.*

OXFORDSHIRE RECORD OFFICE
M2/D – Correspondence relating to the manor of Glympton.

(II) OFFICIAL PRINTED RECORDS

Calendar of Close Rolls.
Calendar of Fine Rolls.
Calendar of Patent Rolls.
John of Gaunt's Register, 1379-83, ed. E.C. Lodge and R. Somerville (2 vols.,
    Camden Society, 3rd series, lvi-lvii, 1937).
Local Government Finance Act 1988.
Rolls of Parliament, (6 vols, London, 1767-77).

(III) CHRONICLES AND LITERARY SOURCES

The Anonimalle Chronicle, 1333–1381, ed. V.H. Galbraith (Manchester
    University Press, 1927).
Anon., *The Garland of Good-Will: Divided Into Three Parts, Containing Many
    Songs and Poems* (London, c.1700).
Anon., *Chronicon Angliae 1328–1388*, ed. E.M. Thompson (*Rolls Series*,
    London, 1874).

John Capgrave, *The Chronicle of England*, ed. F.C. Hingeston (*Rolls Series*, London, 1858).

John Cleveland, *The Idol of The Clownes, or The Insurrections of Wat Tyler, With his Priests Ball and Straw* (London, 1654).

Five Romantic Plays, 1768–1821, ed. P. Baines and E. Burns (Oxford University Press, 2000).

Jean Froissart, *Chronicles of England, France and Spain*, 2 vols, ed. T. Johnes (Routledge, London, 1868).

Gesta Abbatum Monasterii Sancti Albani a Thomas Walsingham, ii-iii, ed. H.T. Riley (*Rolls Series*, London, 1867–9).

Halcot Glover, *Wat Tyler, A Play in Three Acts* (c.1920s).

Historia Angliana, ed. H.T. Riley (2 vols, *Rolls Series*, London, 1863–4).

Knighton's Chronicle, 1337–1396, ed. G.H. Martin (Oxford University Press, 1995).

The Life and Death of Jack Straw, ed. F.P. Wilson (Malone Society Reprint, 1957).

The Riverside Chaucer, ed. L.D. Benson (Oxford University Press, 1988).

William Langland, *The Vision of Piers Plowman*, ed. H.W. Wells and N. Coghill (Sheen and Ward, London, 1935).

Thomas Paine, *The Rights of Man, Common Sense and Other Political Writings*, ed. M. Philip (Oxford University Press, 1998).

G.A. Sala, *Wat Tyler MP, An Operatic Extravaganza*, in *Pantomime and Burlesques*, ii (n.d.).

Wat Tyler: Or, The Prize Fight That Was Settled by a Mace, by D.S., A Historical Burlesque (London, 1867).

The Westminster Chronicle, 1381–1394, ed. L.C. Hector and B.F. Harvey (Oxford, 1980).

SECONDARY SOURCES

(I) PUBLISHED BOOKS AND ARTICLES

Allmand, C., *The Hundred Years War, England and France at War, c.1300–c.1450* (Cambridge University Press, 1989).

Allmand, C., *Henry V* (California University Press, 1992).

Astill, G. and Grant, A., eds, *The Countryside of Medieval England* (Blackwell, Oxford, 1988).

Aston, M., 'The Impeachment of Bishop Despenser', *Bulletin of The Institute of Historical Research*, xxxvii, no. 98 (1965), 127-48.

Aston, T.H., ed., *Landlords, Peasants and Politics in Medieval England* (Cambridge University Press, 1987).

A History of Canterbury Cathedral, ed. P. Collinson, N. Ramsay and M. Sparks (Oxford, 1995).

Barber, R., *Edward Prince of Wales and Aquitaine* (Allen Lane, London, 1978).

Bibliography

Barron, C.M., *Revolt in London: 11th to 15th June 1381*
(London, Museum of London, 1981).

Bellamy, J.G., *The Law of Treason in England in The Late Middle Ages*
(Cambridge University Press, 1970).

Bird, W.H.B., 'The Peasant Rising of 1381, The King's Itinerary', *EHR*, xxi
(1916) 124–5.

Bolton, J.L., *The Medieval English Economy, 1150–1500* (Dent, London, 1980).

Brie, F.W.D., 'Wat Tyler and Jack Straw', *EHR*, xxi (1906), 106–11.

Britnell, R.H., 'Feudal Reaction After the Black Death in the Palatinate
of Durham', *Past & Present*, 128 (1990), 28–47.
The Commercialisation of English Society, 1000–1500 (Cambridge University
Press, 1993).

Brooks, N., 'The Organization and Achievements of the Peasants of Kent
and Essex in 1381', in *Studies in Medieval History Presented to R.H.C.
Davies*, ed. H. Mayr-Harting and R.I. Moore (Hambledon, London, 1985).

Butcher, A.F., 'English Urban Society and the Revolt of 1381', in *The
English Rising of 1381*, ed. Hilton and Aston.

Campbell, B.M.S., ed. *Before the Black Death. Studies in the 'crisis' of the Early
Fourteenth Century* (Manchester University Press, 1991).

Carpenter, D.A., *The Minority of Henry III* (Methuen, London, 1990).

Collins, H.E.J., *The Order of The Garter, 1348-1461: Chivalry and Politics in Late
Medieval England* (Oxford University Press, 2000).

Coulton, G.C., *Medieval Village, Manor and Monastery* (New York, 1960).

Crook, D., 'Derbyshire and the English Rising of 1381', *Historical Research*, lx
no. 141 (1987).

Curry, A., *The Hundred Years' War* (Macmillian, Basingstoke, 1993).

Davis, R.H.C., *King Stephen* (Longmans, London, 1967).

Davies, J.C., 'The Despenser War in Glamorgan', *Transactions of The Royal
Historical Society* (1915).

Davies, R.R., *The Revolt of Owain Glyn Dwr* (Oxford, 1995).

Dobson, R.B., ed., *The Peasants' Revolt of 1381*, 2nd edn
(Macmillan, Basingstoke, 2nd edn 1981).

Dunn, A., 'Wat Tyler: The Many Roles of an English Rebel',
History Today, 51, 7 (July 2001).

Dyer, C.C., 'The Social and Economic Origins of The Great Revolt of
1381', in *The English Rising of 1381*, ed. Hilton and Aston.
*Standards of Living in the Later Middle Ages: Social Change in England,
c.1200–1520* (Cambridge University Press, 1989).
Everyday Life in Medieval England , (Hambledon and London, 1994).

Eiden, H., 'Joint Action against "Bad" Lordship: The Peasants' Revolt in
Essex and Norfolk', *History* 83, no. 269 (1998), 5–30.

Fletcher, A., *Tudor Rebellions* (3rd edn, Longman, London, 1983).

Frazer, J.G., *The Golden Bough, A Study in Religion and Magic*
(abridged edn, Macmillan, London, 1974).

Fryde, E.B., *The Great Revolt of 1381* (Historical Association, London, 1981).
Peasants and Landlords in Later Medieval England, c.1380–c.1525
(Alan Sutton, Stroud, 1996).

Given-Wilson, C., *The Royal Household and The King's Affinity. Service, Politics and Finance in England, 1360–1413* (Yale University Press, 1986).

Given-Wilson, C., ed., *Chronicles of The Revolution, 1397-1400, The Reign of Richard II* (Manchester, 1993).

Goodman, A., *The Loyal Conspiracy*, (Routledge, London, 1971).
John of Gaunt. The Exercise of Princely Power in Europe (Longman, London, 1992).

Goodman, A., and Gillespie, J.L., eds, *Richard II: The Art of Kingship* (Oxford University Press, 1999).

Gottfried, R., *Bury St Edmunds and the Urban Crisis, 1290-1539* (New Jersey, 1982).

Gransden, A., *Historical Writing in England*, ii (Oxford University Press, 1982).

Green, D., *The Black Prince* (Tempus, Stroud, 2001).

Green, R.F., 'John Ball's Letters, Literary History and Historical Literature', in *Chaucer's England, Literature in Historical Context*, ed. B. A. Hanawalt (Minnesota Univ. Press, 1992).

Green, R. F., 'Jack Philpott, John of Gaunt and a Poem of 1380', *Speculum* 66 (1991), 330-41.

Hallam, E.H., *Domesday Book Through Nine Centuries* (Thames and Hudson, London, 1986).

Harding, A., 'The Revolt Against the Justices', in *The English Rising of 1381*, ed. Hilton and Aston.

Harvey, B.F., 'Draft Letters of Manumission and Pardon for the Men of Somerset in 1381', *EHR*, lxxx (1965), 89-91.

Harvey, I.M.W., *Jack Cade's Rebellion of 1450* (Oxford, 1991).

Harvey, I.M.W., 'Was There Popular Politics in Fifteenth-Century England?' *The McFarlane Legacy: Studies in Late Medieval Politics and Society*, ed. R. H. Britnell and A. J. Pollard (Alan Sutton, Stroud, 1995).

Harvey, P.D.A., ed. *The Peasant Land Market in Medieval England* (Oxford, 1984).
A Medieval Oxfordshire Village, Cuxham, 1240–1400 (Oxford University Press, 1965).

Hatcher, J., *Plague, Population and the English Economy, 1348-1530* (Economic Hist. Soc., Macmillan, 1977).

Heath, P., *Church and Realm, 1272–1461, Conflict and Collaboration in an Age of Crisis* (Fontana, London, 1988).

Hill, C., 'The Norman Yoke', reprinted in *Puritanism and Revolution, Studies in Interpretation of the English Revolution of the Seventeenth Century* (Pimlico, London, 2001).

Hilton, R.H., *A Medieval Society. The West Midlands at the End of the Thirteenth Century* (Cambridge University Press, 1966).

Bond Men Made Free, Medieval Peasant Movements and the English Rising of 1381 (Viking, New York, 1973).

The English Peasantry in the Later Middle Ages (Clarendon Press, Oxford, 1975).

The Decline of Serfdom in Medieval England, 2nd edn (Macmillan, London, 1977).

Hilton, R.H., and Aston, T.H., eds, *The English Rising of 1381* (Cambridge University Press, 1984).

Holmes, G.A., *The Good Parliament* (Clarendon Press, Oxford, 1975).

Holt, J.C., *Robin Hood* (London, 1982).

Holt, R., 'Thomas of Woodstock and Events at Gloucester in 1381', *Bulletin of the Institute of Historical Research*, lviii (1985), 237-41.

Holt, R., *The Mills of Medieval England* (Blackwell, Oxford, 1988).

Humphrey, C., *The Politics of Carnival, Festival Misrule in Medieval England* (Manchester, 2001).

Hyams, P. R., *Kings, Lords and Peasants in Medieval England, The Common Law of Villeinage in the Twelfth and Thirteent Centuries* (Oxford, 1980).

Johnson, D.J.J., *Southwark and the City* (Corporation of London, Oxford, 1969).

Jones, M.C.E., *Ducal Brittany 1364–1399* (Oxford University Press, 1970).

Justice, S., *Writing and Rebellion* (London, 1994).

Kenyon, J.P., *The Stuart Constitution, 1603-1688* (Cambridge University Press, 1969).

Leader, D.M., *A History of the University of Cambridge, I, The University to 1546* (Cambridge University Press, 1988).

Liddy, C.D., 'Urban Conflict in Late-Fourteenth Century England: The Case of York In 1380-1', *E.H.R.* cxviii (Feb, 2003), 1-32.

Linebaugh, P., *The London Hanged, Crime and Civil Society in Eighteenth Century England* (Penguin, London, 1991).

Maddicott, J.R., *The English Peasantry and the Demands of the Crown* (*Past and Present Supplement*, 1, Oxford, 1975).

McFarlane, A., *The Origins of English Individualism. The Family, Property and Social Transition* (Blackwell, Oxford, 1978).

McKisack, M., *The Fourteenth Century 1307-1399* (Oxford, 1959).

Miller, E., and Hatcher, J., *Medieval England – Rural Society and Economic Change, 1086-1348* (Longman, London, 1978).

Morgan, M., *The English Lands of The Abbey of Bec* (Oxford, 1946).

Musson, A., 'New Labour Laws, New Remedies? Legal Reaction to the Black Death "Crisis"' in *Fourteenth Century England*, i, ed, N. Saul (Boydell, Woodbridge, 2000).

Oman, C., *The Great Revolt of 1381*, (reprinted, Greenwood, New York, 1969).

Ormrod, W.M., *The Reign of Edward III, Crown and Political Society in England 1327–1377* (Yale, New Haven, 1990).

Ormrod, W. M., 'The Peasants' Revolt and the Government of England', *Journal of British Studies*, 29 (1991).

Ormrod, W. M., and Lindley P. (eds) *The Black Death in England*, (Stamford, 1996).

Palmer, R.C., *English Law in the Age of the Black Death, 1348-1381.*
A Transformation of Governance and Law (Univ. of North Carolina Press, Chapel Hill).

Perroy, E., *The Hundred Years War* (Eyre and Spottiswoode, London, 1959)

Plucknett, T.F.T., *Legislation of Edward I, The Ford Lectures Delivered in the University of Oxford, 1947* (Oxford, 1949).
Edward I and the Criminal Law (Cambridge, 1960).

Postan, M.M., *The Medieval Economy and Society* (Penguin, London, 1972).

Powell, E., *The Rising in East Anglia in 1381* (Cambridge, 1896).

Puttnam, B.H., *The Enforcement of the Statute of Labourers During the First Decade After the Black Death, 1349–1359* (Columbia University, 1908).

Razi, Z., *Life, Marriage and Death in a Medieval Parish. Economy, Society and Demography in Halesowen, 1270–1400* (Cambridge University Press, 1980).

Réville, A., *Etude sur le Soulèvement de 1381 dans les Comtés de Hertford, de Suffolk et de Norfolk* (Paris, 1898).

Roffe, D., *Domesday The Inquest and the Book* (Oxford, 2000).

Saul, N., *Richard II* (Yale University Press, 1997).

Sherborne, J., *War, Politics and Finance in Fourteenth Century England*, ed. A. Tuck (Hambledon, London, 1994).

Smith, J., and Maclean, I., 'The UK Poll Tax and The Declining Electoral Roll: Unintended Consequences?' *Warwick Economic Research Papers*, no.398 (1992).

Stokes, H.P., *University of Cambridge, College Histories, Corpus Christi* (F.E. Robinson, London, 1898).

Storey, R.L., 'The Wardens of The Marches of England Towards Scotland, 1377–1489', *EHR*, lxxii (1957).

Taylor, J., *English Historical Literature in the Fourteenth Century* (Oxford, 1987). Thompson, E.P., *Customs in Common* (Penguin, London, 1991).

Titow, J.Z., *English Rural Society, 1200–1350* (Allen and Unwin, London, 1969).

Towson, K., "Hearts Warped by Passion': The Percy-Gaunt Dispute of 1381', *Fourteenth Century*, iii, ed. W.M. Ormrod (Boydell, Woodbridge, 2003).

Tuck, A., *Richard II and the English Nobility* (Edward Arnold, London, 1973).
'Peasants, Nobles and Commons in The Great Revolt of 1381', in *The English Rising of 1381*, ed. Hilton and Aston.

Vinogradoff, P., *Villainage in England, Essays in Medieval History* (2nd ed., Oxford, 1968).

Walker, S., *The Lancastrian Affinity, 1361-1399* (Oxford, 1990).
'Letters to the Dukes of Lancaster in 1381 and 1399', *EHR*, cvi (1991) 68-79.

Wilkinson, B., 'The Peasants' Revolt of 1381', *Speculum*, xv (1940), 12-35.

Williams, G.A., *Medieval London From Commune to Capital* (University of London, 1963).

Woolgar, C. M., 'Fast and Feast: Conspicuous Consumption and the Diet of the Nobility in the Fifteenth Century', *Revolution and Consumption in Late Medieval England*, ed. M. Hicks (Boydell, Woodbridge, 2001).

(II) THESES

A.J. Prescott, 'Judicial Records of the Rising of 1381' (University of London PhD thesis, 1984).

CHRONOLOGY

1377

January–February	Parliament meets.
	The First Poll Tax granted.
21 June	Death of King Edward III.
24 June	End of truce between England and France.
July	Appointment of Continual Council for the governance of the kingdom.
19 November	John of Gaunt intervenes to halt the trial of John Wycliffe before Bishop Courtenay in St Paul's.
December	Changes to the membership of the Continual Council.

1378

July–September	Unsuccessful campaign of John of Gaunt to capture St Malo.
October	Sir Thomas Trivet's expedition to Navarre.

1379

April	The Second Poll Tax granted.
December	Failed naval expedition of Sir John Arundel.

1380

July	Expedition of army under Thomas, Earl of Buckingham.
16 September	Death of Charles V of France.
November	The Third Poll Tax granted.

1381

January	Royal council resolves to investigate evasion of Third Poll Tax.
16 March	Commissions appointed to recover arrears of Poll Tax.
30 May	Royal commission arrives in Essex to enforce Poll Tax collection.
Sunday 1 June –Tuesday 4 June	Outbreak of disturbances in Kent and Essex.
Monday 10 June	First outbreak of violence in Essex and Kent.
	Attacks on the property of the Hospital of St John in Essex.
	Kentishmen march to Canterbury and occupy the city.
Tuesday 11 June	Richard II, at Windsor, travels by barge to London.
	Elements from the Kentish and Essex rebels march to London.
Wednesday 12 June	Negotiations at Blackheath between the rebels and representatives of the city of London.
	Essex rebels under John Wrawe cross into Suffolk.
	Richard II and his household move to the Tower.
Thursday 13 June	Negotiations between Richard II and the rebels at Greenwich.
	The rebels attack the Marshalsea in Southwark.
	The Savoy Palace and the Temple burned.
	St Albans townsmen present demands to Abbot de la Mare.
	The Suffolk rebels reach Bury St Edmunds.
Friday 14 June	Richard II meets the rebels at Mile End.
	Murder of Archbishop Sudbury and Robert Hales at Tower Hill.
	Massacre of the London Flemings.
	William Grindecobbe travels to London.
	Murder of Sir John Cavendish at Lakenheath.
	First disturbances in Norfolk.
Saturday 15 June	Meeting of Richard II and Wat Tyler at Smithfield.
	Tyler assassinated.
	Royal authority restored in London.
	Execution of Jack Straw?
	Murder of Prior of Bury St Edmunds at Mildenhall.

	Destruction of Cambridge University archives.
	Ransacking of Corpus Christi College.
Sunday 16 June	Escalation of disturbances in St Albans. Abbot de la Mare concedes rebel demands.
	John of Gaunt's wardrobe keeper reaches Leicester to safeguard the ducal possessions.
	Suffolk rebels enter Ipswich.
	Cambridge University forced to surrender privileges to the town.
Monday 17 June	Murder of Justice Edmund Walsingham at Ely.
	Brief rising against Peterborough Abbey.
	Earl of Kent and Sir Thomas Trivet sent to punish rebels in Kent.
Thursday 20 June	Earl of Buckingham and Sir Thomas Trivet commissioned to restore order and punish rebels.
	First commissions sent into East Anglia to restore order.
Saturday 22 June	John of Gaunt flees into Scotland.
Sunday 23 June	Disturbances in Scarborough.
Tuesday 25 June/	
Wednesday 26 June	Defeat of Norfolk rebels at North Walsham by Bishop Despenser.
	Execution of Geoffrey Litster.
Friday 28 June	Defeat of rebels at Billericay by Earl of Buckingham.
Saturday 29 June	Sir Walter atte Lee and his retinue reach St Albans.
2 July	Richard II cancels all of the charters of manumission granted on 14 June.
5 July	Earl of Northumberland sent to restore order in Scarborough.
10 July	John Wrawe tried in London (executed 6 May 1382).
15 July	Execution of John Ball at St Albans.
15 August	Gaunt and Northumberland clash at royal council.
9 October	Gaunt and Northumberland clash again at royal council.
13 October	Execution of William Grindecobbe and leading St Albans rebels.
November	Opening of Parliament.
	Gaunt and Northumberland reconciled formally.

INDEX

Index

Fastolf, Hugh, 85
  Joan, wife of, 85
Felmingham (Norfolk), 161
Ferrers, Sir Ralph, 66, 101
Ferrour, John,
Filmond, Richard, 161
Fitzwalter, Walter, Lord, 169-170
Fleet Street, 105, 116
  Prison, 106
Flemings, massacre of, 113-114, 127
Fobbing (Essex), 94
Fordham, John, Bishop of Durham, Keeper
  of Privy Seal, 100-101, 106, 188
Francis, Adam, 60
Froissart, Jean, 125, 129
Fulham (London), palace, 180

Gartree Hill (Leicester), 150
Gentilhomme, John, 161
Geoffrey, John, 94
Gisburn, John, 87-8, 138
Gissing, Sir Thomas, 160, 165
  Thomas, son of, 160
Gloucester, 170
Glympton (Oxon.), 34, 35
Glyn Dwr, Owain, 22
Gordon, Lord George, 192
Gournay, Edmund, 160
Gower, John, 126
Grantchester, James, 157
  Thomas, 157
Gravesend (Kent), 95
Great Famine (1315-17), 24, 31
Great Ouse, river, 160
Great Wardrobe (London), 125, 128-129
Green, Henry 34
Greenfield, John, 129
Greenwich (Kent), 100, 101, 114, 116, 120
Grindecobbe, William, 78, 141-142, 143,
  154-155, 172-174

Hacking (Norfolk), 169
Haddington (Scotland), 179
Hadleigh (Essex), 169
Hales, Sir Robert, 100-101, 105, 114-115,
  120, 125, 126,
  Sir Stephen, 162
Halesowen (Worcs.), 21
Hanchach, John, 157

Harfleur (France), 54
Harleston, Sir John, 169-170
Haseldene, Thomas, 98
Hatfield, Thomas, Bishop of Durham, 20,
  37, 43
Havering (Essex), 170
Hawley, Robert, 66, 67, 101
Hawkins, Thomas, 35, 42
Henry II (King of England, 1154–1189),
  144-145
Henry III (King of England, 1216–72), 58,
  62
Henry VII (King of England, 1485–1509),
  189-190
Henry of Grosmont, Duke of Lancaster,
  107, 158
Henry of Trastamara, King of Castile, 46,
  54
Hereford, John Gilbert, Bishop of, 179
Hertford, castle, 110, 173
Heryng, Sir Nicholas, 98, 99
Highbury (Middlesex), 105, 106, 141
Hilgay (Norfolk), 160
Hinderclay (Suffolk), 24
Holand, Joan, Duchess of Brittany, 115, 125
  Sir John, 115
  Thomas, Earl of Kent, 115, 120, 169
Holkham, John, 160
Hood, Robin, 190
Holyrood (Edinburgh), 179
Horn, John, 86
Horston Castle (Derbs.), 137-138
Horwood (Herts.), 147
Hothum, Sir John, 178, 179
Hulle, Stephen,

Imworth, Richard, 103-4, 128
Ipswich (Suffolk), 155

Jean II (King of France, 1350–64) 47
Joan of Kent, Princess of Wales, 59, 99, 125
John of Gaunt, Duke of Lancaster, 48, 49,
  52, 53, 54, 61, 62, 64-70, 97-8, 100-
  101, 102-103, 110-111, 115, 138, 158-
  159, 160, 172, 177-182, 184, 193
  Constance, wife of, 177, 178
  Henry, son of, (See Derby, Henry, Earl
  of)

Index